CW01021702

管理智慧篇

唐庆华　著

中國智慧故事

THE BOOK OF CHINESE WISDOM

BOOK I

TIMELESS TALES OF THE ART OF MANAGEMENT

Michael C. Tang

上海人民出版社

送给 nelfie,

　　两套智慧,故事书,有着中国五千年的历史底蕴,是一本帮助外国友人了解中国文化的好书,都望你能喜欢.

好友：张建勇

2009.02

ACKNOWLEDGEMENTS

The Book of Chinese Wisdom was originally published by the Foreign Language Press of Beijing in 1996 under the title of *A Treasury of China's Wisdom*. It was published in the U.S. by Prentice Hall Press in 2000 under the title of *A Victor's Reflections and Other Tales of China's Timeless Wisdom*. Subsequently it was translated into other foreign languages and published in Europe and Asia.

I have completely revised and substantially expanded the book for the bilingual version. The book is now in four volumes, each with a distinct theme.

The Book of Chinese Wisdom is the result of years of studying hundreds of Chinese classics in history, literature and philosophy, ranging from *The Book of Changes* to *Tao Te Ching*, from *The Intrigues of the Warring States* to *The Records of the Historian*, from *Remarks of Monarchs* to *The Comprehensive Mirror to Rulers*, from *The Chronicles of the Three Kingdoms* to *The History of the Ming Dynasty*, traversing the vast panoply of China's history.

In recent years, there is a surge of interest in China. But most newly published books outside China deal with modern China. Few focused on China's classical wisdom. This book is meant to fill that gap. I approach the subject of Chinese classical wisdom with a view of applying it in our present-day life. No prior knowledge of China is needed as I take the reader on a tour through the treasure land of Chinese wisdom and call their attention to the gems in the treasure trove. I hope they will discover the practical value of Chinese wisdom while learning something about Chinese culture.

I am deeply grateful to Wang Meng, former Minister of Culture of China and well-known author, Nicholas Kristof, author and Pulitzer Prize winning journalist of *The New York Times*, Zhu Yinghuang, editor-in-chief emeritus of *China Daily*, and Ross Terrill, well-known author and China scholar at Harvard University, for their generous praise.

At the Shanghai People's Publishing House, I am indebted to Mr. Fan Weiwen and Ms. Pan Danrong for their enthusiasm and thoughtfulness and to Ms. Julia Zhang for her wonderful help.

I owe a special debt to Professor Constance Yang who read the entire manuscript and offered many valuable suggestions that have brightened these pages. I would like to thank Ms. Frances Zhang and Ms. Cecilia Qian for their patience and assistance.

致　谢

　　《中国智慧故事》原用英文撰就，由中国外文出版社于 1996 年出版。2000 年该书由美国最大的出版公司之一普伦蒂斯·霍尔公司在美国出版，随后被译成多种语言在各国出版。

　　作者在撰写英汉对照本的过程中，对原著内容作了全面修订和大幅度的扩充，并拓展为四册。每册有一个主题。

　　《中国智慧故事》是作者根据多年来所研读的数百种中国书籍，包括《老子》、《庄子》、《易经》、《论语》、《左传》、《国策》、《国语》、《史记》、《三国志》、《资治通鉴》等等，选取其中最能代表中国智慧的精华故事，以现代英语重新撰写而成，旨在使不具备中国历史知识的普通英语读者也能了解渊源博大的中国智慧。

　　近年来，世界各国对中国的兴趣日趋浓厚。但是，目前国外出版的多为现代中国的题材，而以普通读者为对象，介绍中国古代智慧的书却极少。其实，中国古典智慧是很有现实意义和实用价值的。作者相信，通过此书，读者既可以受到中国智慧的启迪，又能够增进对中国传统文化的了解。

　　本书渥蒙前文化部长、著名作家王蒙，美国《纽约时报》专栏作家、普利策奖获得者纪思道，英文《中国日报》名誉主编朱英璜，美国著名作家、哈佛大学费正清中心研究员谭若思等撰写赞语，作者深感荣幸。

　　作者十分感谢上海人民出版社对本书的热情支持，特别是范蔚文先生和潘丹榕女士的悉心关怀和指导，以及张玲雅小姐卓有成效的工作。

　　阮式云教授细阅全稿，给我良多助益，我特别感激她。我也感谢张帆小姐和钱华小姐的耐心协助。

　　本书封面之美归功于著名书籍设计师袁银昌先生匠心独运。李静女士的创意也为本书增色无限。本书书名由家父唐清安题写。

The cover is the creation of Mr. Yuan Yinchang, renowned Chinese artist whose works have won domestic and international prizes. Ms. Li Jing has graced the page layout with her ingenuity. The calligraphy was elegantly written by my father with virtuoso brush strokes.

I owe the biggest debt of all to my grandfathers and grandmothers who taught me to love the Chinese classics and cherish their wisdom.

I shall be happy to hear comments and suggestions from my readers.

祖父母和外祖父母从小教我要热爱中国古典精华，珍惜中国智慧。他们是我最应该感谢的人。

作者衷心欢迎读者来信交流心得，并馈赠宝贵意见和建议。

INTRODUCTION

Wisdom is the most precious asset our ancestors have left behind. But it is something that cannot be genetically inherited. Unless we make an effort to learn and practice it, wisdom will not be ours to keep.

The Book of Chinese Wisdom brings together a host of thought-provoking stories that are among the most famous in Chinese classics. They are the gems in the treasure trove of Chinese wisdom. You do not need prior knowledge of Chinese history to appreciate these stories whose morals transcend time and space.

Wisdom is not one-dimensional or singly focused; wisdom is rich in variety and kaleidoscopic in manifestation. *The Book of Chinese Wisdom* is in four volumes. *Book I* is about the art of management; *Book II*'s theme is wit and humor; *Book III* focuses on virtues and values; and *Book IV* contains famous stories of power and influence.

Book I gleans nearly seventy tales of the art of management. With China's long tradition of civil administration, management was a refined art in ancient China. Management, in essence, is about people. Despite advances in science and technology, human nature has hardly changed since ancient times. That is why when I read the stories in the following pages, the practical value of the wisdom embedded therein strike me as fresh and relevant as I first discovered it.

The last part of *Book I* explores the wisdom of *The Book of Changes*. Besides serving as a tool for divination, this classic contains multi-dimensional wisdom. I shall examine the underlying wisdom of its oracles from a business perspective.

序

智慧是祖先留给我们的最宝贵的财富。但是，智慧不能靠基因遗传。如果不努力学习智慧，不运用智慧，我们就无法传承智慧。

《中国智慧故事》搜集了中国历史经典中最著名的故事。这些引人深思的故事是中国智慧宝库里的明珠。读者即使不熟悉中国历史，也能欣赏故事里超越时空的寓意。

智慧层面丰富，种类繁多，表现多姿多彩。《中国智慧故事》共有四册。第一册的主题是管理智慧。第二册的主题是机智与幽默。第三册的重点是教育与伦理。第四册的重点是权谋与兵法。

第一册搜集了近七十个有关管理艺术的故事。中国悠久的文职传统使管理在中国古代就已经成为一门练达的艺术。管理艺术，归根结底，是与人打交道的艺术。今天，尽管科学技术取得了长足的进步，但是人的本性几乎没有变化。这就是为什么当我重温本书故事的时候，我感到这些故事里的智慧既新鲜又实用，就像我第一次发现它们时那样。

本书的最后部分探讨了《易经》的智慧。《易经》不仅是占卜的工具，它的智慧有许多层面。在本书中，笔者将从管理角度来探讨《易经》的智慧。

CONTENTS   目录

Part I Managing Yourself   管理自我

Part II Managing Your Boss   管理上司

Part III   Managing Subordinates   管理下属

2

Part IV   Managing Human Resources   管理人才资源

Part V Managing Opponents   管理对手

CONTENTS 目录

Part VI Wisdom of *The Book of Changes* 《易经》的管理智慧

PART I

MANAGING YOURSELF

管理自我

1

THE HANDSOME MAN

Zou Ji, prime minister of Qi, was a handsome man. One day as he was straightening his clothes in front of a mirror before going to the court, he asked his wife, "Who do you think is more handsome, me or Lord Xu?"

"Of course, it's you, my lord," said his wife.

But Zou Ji was not sure because Lord Xu was well-known for his handsome look. So he put the question to his maid.

"Who is better-looking, me or Lord Xu?"

"Lord Xu can't compare with Your Lordship," came the maid's reply.

The following day Zou Ji asked a guest, "Between Lord Xu and I, who do you think is better looking?"

"Lord Xu is nowhere near so handsome as Your Excellency," said the guest.

A few days later Lord Xu himself called upon him. Looking at his visitor up close, Zou Ji decided that Lord Xu was definitely more handsome. There was no doubt about it.

He thought to himself, "My wife says I am better looking because she loves me; my maid says I am better looking because she is afraid of me; my guest says the same thing because he is asking a favor of me."

Then he had an audience with the king.

"I am not as handsome as Lord Xu," he said to the king,

1
邹忌谏齐王

　　齐相邹忌相貌英俊。一天早上，上朝前，他穿戴好衣帽，照着镜子，问妻子："我和城北徐公相比，谁更英俊？"

　　他妻子说："当然是你。"

　　城北徐公是齐国有名的美男子。邹忌不相信自己能跟徐公相比，就问妾："我和徐公哪个更英俊？"

　　妾答："徐公哪里有老爷美呢？"

　　第二天，有客人来，邹忌问客人："我和徐公比，谁更英俊？"

　　客人说："徐公肯定不如阁下英俊。"

　　几天后，徐公本人来访。邹忌仔细观察了他，觉得自己比徐公差得多。他想，妻子说我比徐公美，是因为她爱我；妾说我比徐公美，是因为她怕我；客人说我比徐公美，是因为有求于我。

　　于是，他上朝时对齐王说："臣明明知道自己不如徐公美，但臣的妻、妾、客人都说我比徐公美。大王是一国之主。宫妃左右没有不偏袒你的；朝廷大臣没有不怕你的；四方境内没有不有求于你的。你受的蒙蔽一定

"yet my wife, my maid, and my guest all told me that I am better looking than him. Your Majesty is a powerful man. No court lady is not partial to you; no official is not afraid of you; everybody hopes to get something from you. Think of the consequences if you were deluded by flattery."

The king took his point. He issued a decree to the effect that any official or ordinary citizen who pointed out his faults to his face would be awarded first prize; anyone who did so by writing to him would be awarded second prize, and anyone who criticized him in public would be given third prize.

Within days so many people responded to his call that the gate of the palace became as crowded as a marketplace. A few months later, people still came forward with suggestions to improve on the government. After a year, no one could find anything to criticize, though people were still eager to win a prize.

4

COMMENT: The more powerful you are, the less likely that people around you will tell you the truth, and the more likely you will make mistakes.

很厉害。"

齐王说："你的话很有道理。"于是他颁布诏令：齐国臣民凡是能当面指出齐王过错的，可以得到上赏；凡是能上书直谏齐王过错的，可以得到中赏；凡是能在街头巷尾批评齐王过错的，可以得到下赏。

诏令刚一公布，臣民争相谏诤，王宫前门庭若市。数月后，还有人向朝廷进言。一年以后，许多人即使想得到赏赐，也没有什么意见可提了。

点评：你的权力越大，周围的人就越不会对你说真话，你就越容易犯错误。

子
zǐ
child; son

此字原像一个四肢伸开的婴儿，但后来婴儿的腿用襁褓包住了。
The original character depicted an infant with outstretched arms and legs. Later the legs were swaddled in cloth bands.

2

SELF-RESTRAINT

As envoy of the king of Zhao, Lin Xiangru scored a series of diplomatic victories in dealing with the king of Qin thanks to his uncommon courage and resourcefulness. The king of Zhao was so pleased he appointed him chief minister, a position more senior than that held by Chief General Lian Po, the country's highest-ranking army officer.

Consequently General Lian Po bore Lin Xiangru a grudge. "I did much more for the country than Lin Xiangru," he complained. "All he did was wagging his tongue. How come he has a higher rank? When I see him, I'll give him a piece of my mind."

When Lin Xiangru heard of his remark, he made a point of keeping himself out of the general's way. He even pretended illness so as to avoid meeting him in the court. One day he was riding in his carriage when he saw General Lian Po coming in the opposite direction, he ordered his driver to quickly turn into an alley until the general went past.

"Why are you so afraid of him?" asked his aides. "You hold a higher position, but you act as though you were inferior to him. You made us feel ashamed."

"Who is more formidable, the king of Qin or General Lian Po?" asked Lin Xiangru.

2

将 相 和

　　蔺相如作为赵王的使臣，出使秦国，机智勇敢地赢得了一系列外交上的胜利。赵王极为高兴，就拜他为上卿，地位在赵国最高的将领廉颇之上。这可引起了廉颇的强烈不满。

　　廉颇生气地说："我的功劳远比蔺相如大。他只靠一张嘴，就爬到我头上来了。只要我碰到他，非给他颜色看看不可。"

　　他的话传到蔺相如的耳朵里，蔺相如就竭力回避廉颇，甚至装病不去上朝，免得跟廉颇碰面。有一天，蔺相如的马车在街上走，远远看见廉颇的马车从对面过来。蔺相如连忙叫车夫把车子赶到路旁的小巷里躲起来，等到廉颇的车子走了才出来。

　　他的随从问他："您干吗那么怕他？您的地位比他高，您干吗老是低声下气的？我们咽不下这口气。"

　　蔺相如说："你们说廉颇将军同秦王哪个厉害？"

　　"当然是秦王。"

　　蔺相如说："我蔺某人秦王都不怕，怎么会害怕廉颇呢？秦国不敢侵犯赵国，是因为有我和廉颇这样的人

"Of course, the king of Qin."

"Just think of it," explained the chief minister, "I'm not afraid of the king of Qin, would I be afraid of Lian Po? Qin dare not invade Zhao because people like Lian Po and I are serving in the government. If the two of us start fighting like two tigers, one is bound to perish. For the interest of the country I must swallow my pride."

His words reached General Lian Po's ears. Baring his shoulders and carrying a thorny switch on his back, he called on Lin Xiangru to apologize.

"Please forgive me, Your Honor," he spoke as he knelt down. "You have a big heart; but I am an ignorant boor. I'm ashamed of my behavior. I deserve to be whipped with a thorny switch."

Lin Xiangru got down on his knees too. "General, I do appreciate your understanding. Let's work together for the country."

His words brought tears to the general's eyes. The two men embraced each other and became great friends.

COMMENT: What made the reconciliation possible was not only both men were innately decent but they shared a purpose larger than their own ego.

在。如果我们两人发生冲突，两虎相斗，必有一伤。为
了国家的利益，我必须咽下这口气。"

他的话传到廉颇的耳朵里后，廉颇打着赤膊，背上
荆条，直奔蔺相如府上去请罪。

他跪在地上，对蔺相如说："实在对不起您啊。您
是那样宽宏大量。我是个粗人。我为自己的行为感到惭
愧。我应当受到荆条鞭笞。"

蔺相如也跪了下来。"将军能体谅我的苦心，我很
感激。让我们一起为国家出力吧。"

廉颇感动得直流眼泪。从此以后，两人成为生死与
共的知心朋友。

点评：廉颇和蔺相如之所以能和解，不仅是因为两个人都有好品德，而且是因
为他们都有一个比自尊心更大的共同目标。

3

"I DON'T WANT TO KNOW"

When Lu Mengzheng was appointed deputy prime minister by Taizong, the second emperor of the Song dynasty, he was only in his thirties. One day at a ministerial meeting, he happened to walk past a man who was making a sarcastic remark about him, "Is that greenhorn the new deputy prime minister?"

Lu Mengzheng pretended not to have heard anything. But an associate of his heard it and got angry. He wanted to find out the man's name. Lu Mengzheng stopped him.

"It's better not to ask," Lu Mengzheng said. "If I know the man's name, I may never forget. If I don't, I have nothing to vex my mind."

COMMENT: You can choose what to know and what not to know as well as choose your response.

3

吕蒙正处世

当吕蒙正被宋太宗任命为副宰相时，他只有三十多岁。一天，他上朝开会，走过一个人身旁，那人挖苦地说了一句："这个小子居然也参政？"

吕蒙正装作没听见。可是他的同僚听见了，气不过，要查出说话人的姓名。吕蒙正制止了他。

他说："还是不问的好。我如果知道这人的姓名，可能一辈子都不会忘记。如果不知道，我就没有什么烦恼。"

点评：你可以选择想知道什么，不想知道什么，以及选择你的反应。

4

ONE-UPMANSHIP

Wang Dan was the highest ranking military officer under Emperor Zhenzong in the Song dynasty. One day, Kou Zhun, a talented colleague of his, called upon him and asked him to help him secure the position of a regional prefect which would put him in charge of several provinces.

Wang Dan gave Kou Zhun a disapproving look. "Regional prefect is an important post. How can you ask for it as though it's a private favor? I never use my office for private favor."

Kou Zhun bore him a grudge for the snub. Not long afterwards the emperor appointed Kou Zhun to the post he desired and he was very grateful.

"If it's not for Your Majesty, I would not have been so fortunate."

"No, it's not my idea," the emperor told him. "Wang Dan recommended you."

Kou Zhun was ashamed. Later Wang Dan recommended him to be prime minister. Yet Kou Zhun often spoke ill of Wang Dan to the emperor while Wang Dan had only praise for him.

"You speak highly of Kou Zhun," the emperor told Wang Dan, "but he only talks about your faults."

"It's natural," replied Wang Dan. "I've been in office a

4

王旦的器量

王旦是宋真宗时的太尉。有一次，寇准私下去王旦家，要求做节度使。寇准颇有才能，王旦却不以为然地说："节度使这样重要的职位你怎么能够私下请求呢？我从不接受私人的请托。"

寇准因此怀恨在心。过了不久，诏书下来任命寇准为节度使。

寇准非常感激皇上。他对皇上说："要不是陛下知臣，臣怎么可能受此恩宠呢？"

皇上说："这不是我的主意，是王旦推荐你的。"

寇准感到很惭愧。后来王旦又推荐他做宰相。可是寇准经常在真宗面前数落王旦的不是，而王旦则专说寇准的优点。

真宗对王旦说："你老是说寇准的好话，但他专门挑你的毛病。"

王旦说："这是理所当然的。臣在位时间久了，工作上一定有许多不足之处。寇准批评我，表明他对皇上忠诚，这也是我看中他的原因。"

真宗越发尊重王旦。寇准尽管地位很高，但他总觉

long time. I had my share of mistakes. Kou Zhun criticized me out of loyalty to Your Majesty. That is why I think favorably of him."

The emperor held Wang Dan in greater respect. Despite his exalted position, Kou Zhun always felt inferior to Wang Dan.

COMMENT: Kou Zhun might have the ability to be prime minister but certainly not the broad mind to be a good one.

得自己比不上王旦。

点评：寇准或有宰相之才，可是没有做一个好宰相的度量。

女
nǚ
woman; girl

最早的女字像一个双手放在前面、跪在地上的女子。这说明古代女子的地位很低。

The original pictograph depicted a kneeling woman with arms holding in front of her body. This tells us that the status of a woman was low in ancient times.

5

CAREER MANAGEMENT

Du Yan was prime minister under Emperor Renzong in the Song dynasty. One day a former student of his visited him before leaving the capital to take the position of a county magistrate.

"Your talent is well above the requirements for a county magistrate," Du Yan told the young man, "but to make a success of your career, you must keep a low profile, stay in the middle and refrain from showing your smarts. Otherwise you'll get into trouble."

"What do you mean, Master?" the student asked. "You are respected by everyone for being outspoken and faithful. Why did you tell me to lie low?"

"I've been in the bureaucracy long enough," Du Yan explained. "I've held many offices. The emperor knows me; my colleagues trust me. Therefore I was able to do a lot of things and fulfill my ambition. You are a mere county magistrate. Your promotion depends on those above you. If I don't give you the benefit of my experience, you can cause trouble for yourself. If that happens, you may never realize your aspirations. That's why I advise you not to be too sharp, too rash, but to stay steady in the middle."

COMMENT: Like it or not, your advancement often hinges on how you handle office politics—it is a subtle art that is vital to your career success.

5

杜衍告诫门生

杜衍是宋仁宗时的宰相。有一天，一位门生当上县令，离京赴任前去看他。

杜衍告诫门生说："你的才能当一个县令是绰绰有余的。但是，你要成功就要善于韬晦，不要锋芒太露，稳居中游就可以了。不然的话，不但无益于事，反而会取祸。"

门生问："老师平生忠诚直率，因而受到天下人的敬重。为什么今天反而叫学生韬光养晦呢？"

杜衍说："我历任的官职多，做官的时间也长，上为皇帝所知，下为朝野所信，因此才得以伸展我的志向。你现在只是一个小小的县令。官运的好坏取决于你的上级官吏。如果我不告诉你我的经验，你只会徒然取祸。如何能够伸展平生的抱负呢？所以，我要你磨去棱角，稳居中游，不要冒进。"

点评：不管你喜欢不喜欢，你的职场升迁取决于你如何处理好与同事和上下级的关系。人际关系的处理对于职业生涯的成功是一门很重要的艺术。

6

TREES

One day Xi Simi, a government minister in Qi, called upon Viscount Tian Cheng, the most powerful man in the country. He was taken to a tower to look at the scenery. The view was splendid except that it was obstructed in the south by the trees grown in the garden of Xi Simi's house. The viscount said nothing.

When he got home, Xi Simi ordered his servants to chop the trees down. Just as they started cutting, he stopped them.

"Why did you change your mind, sir?" his aide asked.

"The viscount is working on a secret scheme. If he knew I could read his mind, I would be in danger. Not to cut down the trees won't be much of an offense but knowing something that he does not like me to know will have serious consequences."

COMMENT: Knowing too much can be just as bad as knowing too little. And there are times when it is better to hide what you know.

6

隰斯弥砍树

隰斯弥是齐国的大臣。有一天，他谒见齐国最有权势的人田成子。田成子带他登上一个高台，眺望风景。三面的景致都很秀丽，只有向南面望去时，隰斯弥家的树木遮住了他们的视线。田成子什么也没说。

隰斯弥回到家里，便命令仆人把树砍掉。但他们刚砍了几下，隰斯弥又叫他们停下来。

隰斯弥的家臣问他："为什么你改变了主意？"

隰斯弥说："田成子正在酝酿一项秘密的计划。如果他知道我能够猜透他的心思，我就会有危险。不砍掉树木，没有罪过。知道人家不愿让你知道的心思，后果可就严重了。"

点评：知道得太多和知道得太少都不好。有的时候，你最好掩饰所知道的事。

7

DOMAIN OF PRIME MINISTER

Bing Ji was prime minister under Emperor Xuan of the Han dynasty. One day he and his aides were riding through the capital when they came upon a scene of street fight. Bodies of the injured and the dead were lying in the streets. But Bing Ji passed by without saying a word. His aides were perplexed.

Going a little further, Bing Ji saw a man driving an ox. The ox was panting with its tongue sticking out. Bing Ji stopped to chat with the man, asking him how far he had traveled. His aides thought he had lost his sense of proportion, querying about small things and ignoring big ones.

Bing Ji replied, "It's the duty of the magistrate of Chang'an and municipal officials to deal with street fights. The prime minister should not get involved. It would not be appropriate for me to stop in the street to make inquiries. My duty is to review their performance, deciding whether they've done a good job, and then make recommendation to the emperor for promotion or demotion. Now is spring time. But it is hot. If an ox is gasping after walking only a few miles, it may indicate unseasonable weather. This is serious because harvest could be affected. The people's livelihood is at stake. That's why I stopped to talk to the man."

COMMENT: If you exceed your mandate and meddle in areas that are the responsibility of others, more often than not, you would do a thankless job.

7

丙吉为相

丙吉是汉宣帝时的丞相。有一次他和下属外出，正好碰到街上有人打群架。一些被打死打伤的人躺在地上。但丙吉经过，问也不问一下。他的下属感到很奇怪。

再往前走，他们碰到一个人在赶牛，牛舌头吐在外面，喘息不止。丙吉停下马车，问那个赶牛人赶这牛走了多远了。下属感到很奇怪，觉得丙吉大事不问，小事却问个明白。就请教他是什么缘故。

丙吉说："处理老百姓群斗，是长安府的职责，不关丞相的事。我在路上停下来问这些事不合适。我的任务是考核官员们的政绩，然后奏请皇上加以赏罚。现在正当春天，不应该这么热。这头牛走路不多，却喘大气，说明气候不正常，收成可能受影响，老百姓的生活可能受影响。所以我停下来问那赶牛的人。"

点评：如果你超越职权，干涉属于他人权责范围内的事，往往会吃力不讨好。

8

TRANSGRESSION

When Zilu, a disciple of Confucius, was the magistrate of Hou, the ruler of Lu conscripted laborers to dig canals for the purpose of preventing waterlogging. One day, seeing some laborers go hungry, Zilu prepared food for them at his own expense. But Confucius sent Zigong, a fellow disciple, to stop him.

"Did I do something wrong?" Zilu demanded angrily when he called upon Confucius. "Didn't you tell us to be charitable?"

"You are too naive," Confucius said. "I thought you understood politics. These men were hired by the ruler of Lu. If they have no food, you ought to report to the ruler of Lu who can open the granary for the purpose. Your intention is good, but you are overstepping your authority."

Hardly had Confucius finished his words when an envoy of the ruler of Lu came.

He asked Confucius, "Are you trying to buy popularity by sending your disciple to distribute food to these workers? What is your intention?"

COMMENT: Zilu did not realize even if he emptied his own pocket, he would not be able to feed these laborers. If the laborers did not get their food in time, reporting to the ruler of Lu would help set up a system to fix the problem. And a system is always stronger than an individual.

22

8

越　权

　　子路当郈城令时，鲁君征发民夫挖掘水沟防涝。子路看见民夫挨饿，就拿出自己的俸米，煮了饭给民工吃，孔子听说后，就派子贡去阻止他。

　　子路跑到孔子那里，愤愤地质问他："老师一直教导我们要行仁义，我什么地方做错了？"

　　孔子说："你太天真了。我还以为你懂得政治呢！民工是鲁君雇用的。他们没有粮食吃，你应该向鲁君禀报，从国库里拿出粮食来。你的用心是好的，但你的做法是越权的。"

　　话音未落，鲁君的使者就来到孔子那里，责问孔子："先生让弟子煮饭给民工吃，是想收买民心。你有什么目的？"

点评：子路没有认识到，即使他倾其所有，也未必能使民工吃饱。禀报鲁君有助于建立一套制度来解决问题。制度的力量总是比个人大。

9

DOG AT WINESHOP

There was a wine seller whose wine was good and whose price reasonable. However, he had few customers. Puzzled, he asked his neighbor for advice.

"Your business is poor because you have a fierce dog," the neighbor said.

"But wine is wine, dog is dog. They have nothing to do with each other."

"You are wrong. Whenever a customer comes to your shop, your dog barks at him. The customer is scared and goes away. As long as you keep that dog, few dare to come to your shop and your wine will turn sour."

Guan Zhong, prime minister of Qi, used this fable to warn Duke Huan about bad men who were close to a ruler. They controlled the access to the ruler, kept him in the dark and kept good men away. The existence of such people put the country at risk.

COMMENT: Those in position of authority should watch out for people around them who may resemble the dog at the wineshop.

9

狗 与 酒

　　有一个卖酒的，酒做得很好，价钱也很公道，可就是顾客很少。

　　他觉得奇怪，就问邻居。

　　邻居说："你生意不好，是因为你家有一条恶狗。"

　　"可是狗归狗，酒归酒，两者之间没有什么关系啊。"

　　"你错了。顾客来你的店买酒，你的狗迎上去冲着他叫。人家害怕了，就走了。只要你养着这条恶狗，就很少有人敢上门，你的酒也会变酸。"

　　齐相管仲用这个寓言来提醒齐桓公提防君主左右的坏人。这种人控制君主能见哪些人，不见哪些人。他们掩蔽君主的耳目，不让好人接近君主。有他们在，国家就有危险。

点评：当权者应该注意自己的身边是不是有像酒店里的恶狗那样的人。

10

COMMITMENT

Jiang and Huang were two small states located close to the powerful state of Chu. When Chu threatened to annex them, both sent envoys to Qi to seek an alliance with Duke Huan, the ruler of Qi.

"Don't acquiesce in their request," Prime Minister Guan Zhong advised the duke. "These two states are too far away. If Chu attacks them, we won't be able to defend them. If we become their ally but can't live up to our commitment, we'll lose our credibility."

But Duke Huan ignored his warning. He went ahead and formed the alliance. When Chu attacked Jiang and Huang, Qi could not come to their rescue in time, and they were eventually subjugated by Chu. As a result, the prestige of Duke Huan plummeted, and countries that had previously held him in high regard no longer listened to him.

COMMENT: Never commit yourself beyond your ability. Credibility is easy to lose, hard to gain and even harder to regain.

10

齐桓公失信

江国和黄国是两个小国家，离楚国很近。楚国是大国，几次想出兵消灭这两个国家。于是，江国和黄国派使者到齐国，想跟齐桓公结盟。

齐相管仲向齐桓公建议说："不要接受他们的要求。这两个国家离齐国太远了。如果楚国攻打他们，我们没有能力援救。如果我们做了他们的盟友，却不能履行承诺，我们就没法交代了。"

但齐桓公没听管仲的话，还是和江、黄两国结了盟。当楚国攻打这两个国家时，齐国无法及时援救。结果，它们被楚国消灭了。

从此以后，齐桓公的威信扫地。以前尊重他的各国不再听他的话了。

点评：没有能力做到的事，千万不可贸然承诺。建立信用很难，失去信用很容易，失去以后重建信用难上加难。

11

THE FIDDLE

When Chen Zi-ang first came to Chang'an, the capital of the Tang dynasty, nobody knew him. He passed the imperial examination, but it was no big deal as hundreds of others did the same. Chen Zi-ang was frustrated.

One day he was strolling in the streets when he saw a man selling a fiddle. The asking price was a thousand ounces of gold. A big crowd gathered around, but nobody knew whether the instrument was worth the price. Chen Zi-ang pushed his way through to the front.

"I'll buy it," he told the seller. "Come with me."

The crowd stared at him in astonishment.

"Do you play the fiddle, sir?" someone asked.

"Yes. I'm a virtuoso player," replied Chen Zi-ang.

"Could you play for us, please?"

"Sure. Come to the square in front of the Temple of the Town God tomorrow morning. I'll play for you."

The next day many people gathered there. Holding the fiddle in his hand, Chen Zi-ang announced, "I am a scholar from Sichuan. I've passed the imperial examination, but nobody cares. I would like you to read my writings. As for the fiddle, I don't know how to play it. I'm not interested in being a fiddler."

With that, he smashed the fiddle. Then he handed out

11

陈子昂扬名计

当陈子昂初到唐朝京城长安时，谁也不认得他。虽然他考中进士，但考中进士也没有什么了不起，因为每年科举总有上百人中进士。陈子昂很丧气。

有一天，他在街上看到一个人在卖胡琴。胡琴的要价高达一千两金子。围观的人很多，但谁也不知道这把胡琴到底值不值这个价钱。

陈子昂推开人群走到前面。他告诉卖琴的人："这把胡琴我买了，你跟我来。"

大家吃惊地看着他。有人问："先生喜欢拉胡琴吗？"

"我是拉胡琴的高手。" 陈子昂回答说。

"可否请先生拉一曲给我们听听？"

"当然可以。请你们明天早上到城隍庙前的广场上来，我拉给你们听。"

第二天，很多人聚集在那里。陈子昂举着那把胡琴，对大家说："我是从四川来的一个读书人，刚考中进士，可是没有人欣赏我。我想请大家读读我写的文章。至于拉胡琴，我不会，我也不想当乐工。"

说着，他就把那把昂贵的胡琴摔破了。大家正在惊

copies of his essay to the astonished spectators. Soon enough his reputation spread. Before long even Empress Wu heard of him. She gave him an audience and offered him a good position in the government. Later Chen Zi-ang became a well-known poet.

COMMENT: Using unconventional means to court publicity is fine provided you have real talent. If you don't, you will expose yourself to ridicule.

愕之中，陈子昂把事先准备好的文稿发给他们。没多久，他的名声就传遍京师，连武则天皇后都知道了。武则天召见了他，让他在朝廷担任要职。后来，陈子昂成为一名大诗人。

点评：用非常规手段为自己博取名声的前提是你必须有真才实学。如果你没有真才实学，那只会被人嗤笑。

好
hǎo
good; nice

一个女子抱着她的孩子，构成了一幅美好的图画。
A woman holding a baby forms a good picture.

12

THE REAL THING

Lord Ye was so fond of dragons he took to wearing clothes embroidered in dragon pattern, drank wine from a cup carved with dragons, and lived in a house decorated with paintings of dragons.

When a real dragon heard of his passion, it came down from the sky to call on Lord Ye. As it stuck its head through a window into the lord's room to make an effort to befriend him, its appearance so frightened Lord Ye that he fled into the street, dashing aside all obstacles, as though he was running for his life.

COMMENT: People may not be what they claim to be. Lord Ye is only fond of what looks like a dragon, not real dragons. Indeed we ourselves may sometimes behave like him, that is, being dishonest to ourselves.

12

叶公好龙

叶公喜欢龙。他穿的衣物上绣着龙，用的酒杯上雕着龙，住的房子里也画满了龙。

真的龙听说叶公这么喜欢龙，就从天上飞到他家，把头伸进窗户，想和叶公交个朋友。叶公见到龙，吓得六神无主，没命似地逃到街上。

点评：人们往往并不像他们自己所说的那样。叶公不是喜欢真的龙，他喜欢的只是像龙的东西。其实，我们有时候也可能像叶公那样，那就是对自己不诚实。

孕
yùn
pregnant

此字外部是身体，里面是婴儿。
This ideograph consists of a human body outside and a fetus inside.

PART II

MANAGING YOUR BOSS

管理上司

1

REWARD OR NO REWARD

Yan Ying was the governor of Dong'e. Three years into his term, there were so many complaints about him that Duke Jing, the ruler of Qi, decided to relieve him of his post.

"I've realized my mistakes now, Your Highness," said Yan Ying. "If you let me stay on for another three years, I promise I will improve."

Three years later, indeed there was much commendation about him. The duke was so pleased he summoned him to the court to be rewarded, but Yan Ying declined the honor.

"When I went to Dong'e the first time," he said, "I cleaned up corruption in the government. Those who were affected resented me. I punished criminals. Law-breakers hated me. I refused to give special consideration to the rich and influential. They were offended. When those around me asked for a favor, I only gave them what was legally allowed. They were displeased. When I entertained my superiors, I never exceeded the limit of normal standards. My superiors did not like that. All of them heaped slanders on me.

"In the last three years, I changed my way of doing things. No more clamp-down on corruption. No more punishment for those who broke the law. Whatever those around me asked for, I granted with a smile. Special consideration was given to

1

晏婴治东阿

晏婴治理东阿县三年，有很多人说他的坏话。齐景公决定撤掉他的官职。

晏婴说："主公，我知道自己的过错了。请让我再治理三年，我保证进步。"

三年后，齐景公果然听到很多人说晏婴的好话。这下他高兴了，就召晏婴入朝，要封赏他。晏婴谢绝了。

他说："以前我在东阿做官时，我整治官场腐败，贪官污吏怨恨我；我打击犯罪，犯法的人怨恨我；我没有特别照顾有钱有势的人，他们生我的气；周围的人有求于我，不合法的要求我不答应，他们不高兴；招待上司时，我不超过礼制的规定，上级也不喜欢我。这些人到处诽谤我。

"最近这三年，我改弦更张。我不惩治腐败；不打击犯罪；周围的人有什么请求，我欣然满足；有钱有势的人，我特别照顾；招待上司，我百般殷勤。所以，这些人都赞扬我。其实，我前三年该受封赏，后三年该受惩罚。所以，我不能接受主公的奖赏。"

齐景公恍然大悟，于是委任晏婴为相国。在晏婴的

REWARD OR NO REWARD

the rich and influential. And I treated my superiors with lavish hospitality. As a result, all of them said good things about me.

"Frankly, I should have been rewarded for what I did in my first three years and punished for what I did in the last three years. That's why I can't accept any reward."

Duke Jing was struck. He appointed Yan Ying prime minister and Qi became a very prosperous country under Yan Ying's management.

COMMENT: Sometimes taking a step back is better than taking a step forward for achieving your objective. Yan Ying helped Duke Jing discern between right and wrong by temporarily retreating from principle.

治理下，齐国兴盛起来。

点评：有时候退比进更能达到目的。晏婴暂时放弃原则，而终于达到了帮助齐
景公分清是非的目的。

安
ān
peace; stable

此字上部象征家。古人相信，有一个女子在家料理家
务，做男人的生活就会安定。
The upper part of the character stands for a house and the lower
part is a woman. It means a man will have a stable life if he has a
woman to take care of the house.

2

THE INTERPRETATION OF A DREAM

Duke Jing of Qi fell ill with edema, a disease caused by an excess of body fluid. He had a dream one night in which he was beaten by two suns in a fight.

The following morning he told his prime minister Yan Ying about his dream and asked whether it was not an omen of his death.

"Your Highness should consult a dream interpreter," said Yan Ying. "Let me get you one."

When the dream interpreter came, Yan Ying met him at the entrance of the palace and told him about the duke's dream.

"I have to go home and consult my book." the dream interpreter said.

Yan Ying stopped him. "No, it's not necessary. The duke's illness is caused by too much body fluid. Body fluid is water; water represents *yin*. He was defeated by two suns in his dream. The sun is the source of light and heat; it represents *yang*. Now *yin* was defeated by *yang* in his dream. So the duke should get well soon. Just tell him that."

The dream interpreter thought Yan Ying's explanation made perfect sense and so he told the duke as much. A few days later the duke recovered. He wanted to reward the dream interpreter.

2

晏婴释梦

　　齐景公患了水肿，体内湿气过盛。夜里，他梦见自己跟两个太阳打架，结果被打败了。

　　第二天，他对相国晏婴说起这个梦，问他这是不是死亡的预兆。

　　晏婴回答说："这事主公应该问占梦的。让我召一个占梦者进宫来。"

　　占梦者到达后，晏婴在王宫门口见了他，告诉了他齐景公的梦。

　　占梦的说："我得回去查考一下占梦的书才能解释。"

　　晏婴说："不必了。主公的病是因为体内湿气太多，有积水。水属于阴。他梦见被两个太阳打败。太阳发光发热，属于阳。主公的梦里，一阴不胜二阳，说明他的病快要好了。你就这么告诉他。"

　　占梦者认为晏婴的解释合情合理，于是就照样对景公说了。没几天，景公的病果然好了。他要赏赐占梦者。

　　占梦者说："这不是臣的功劳,是晏婴教臣这么说的。"

　　但是，晏婴不肯接受赏赐。他说："虽然梦是我解释的，但是，如果从我嘴里说出来，主公未必相信。占

"No, I don't deserve a reward," the man said. "Your Highness should reward Yan Ying because it was he who told me how to interpret your dream."

But Yan Ying would not accept the reward. "Although the interpretation was mine," he said, "if I had told Your Highness myself, you wouldn't have believed it. It was the dream interpreter who convinced you. So I don't think I should take the credit."

The duke rewarded both men.

COMMENT: The messenger is as important as the message.

梦者说了，主公就相信了。所以我没有功劳。"

最后，齐景公两个人都给了赏赐。

点评：传递信息的人和信息本身一样的重要。

43

夫
fū
husband

此字在"人"字上加两横。古代男子到了 20 岁，就束发戴帽，表示已经成年。
The character came from the word for man. In ancient times, when a man reached twenty, he must bind his hair with a hairpin and put on a cap to indicate manhood.

3

APPOINTMENT

King Wu, founder of the Zhou dynasty, called upon a venerable elder of the Shang dynasty which he had overthrown. He wanted to know the man's opinion about Shang's fall. The elder made an appointment with him the following day to discuss.

King Wu went there with his brother, but the man never showed up. The king was upset. His brother had an inspiration.

"I understand. The man used to serve in the Shang court. He is unwilling to criticize his dead king before a conqueror."

"Then why did he make the appointment?"

"He made the appointment yet did not show up. He is telling you the reason Shang had fallen: the king of Shang had failed to keep his promise to the people and consequently lost their support. I believe that is the message he wants to convey to you."

COMMENT: A simple yet sophisticated mode of communication.

3

失　约

　　周武王推翻商朝以后，前去拜见商朝的一位长者，问他商朝亡国的原因。长者和他约定第二天见面再谈。

　　周武王和他的弟弟第二天去赴约，可是，那位长者却没有来。周武王很不高兴。他的弟弟恍然大悟。

　　他对周武王说："我明白了。这位长者曾在商王的朝廷供职。他不愿意在一个征服者面前批评他的国君。"

　　"那么，他为什么约我见面呢？"

　　"他约你见面，却不来，就等于告诉你，商朝亡国的原因是商王因为失信于民而丧失了人民的支持。这就是他想传达给你的信息。"

点评：这是一个简单然而相当巧妙的传达信息的方式。

4

BAD NEWS

Li Hang was prime minister under Emperor Zhenzong in the Song dynasty. Whenever he was given an audience, he always brought up bad news such as the crime rate in the country, the decline of social morals, natural disasters and so on. The emperor was so displeased that his face would change color.

"Why do you always talk about bad things?" Li Hang's colleagues demanded. "We are living in a time of peace. Aren't we lucky enough to hold office? The issues you raised are being handled by various officials. Is it necessary to tell the emperor about them and make him unhappy? If you insist on reporting them, it is better to report after they have been dealt with."

"I disagree," Li Hang said. "I want to make sure that the emperor has things to worry about. If he is free from all anxieties, he may indulge himself and lose self-discipline."

COMMENT: A sense of anxiety is necessary to keep a man from being complacent.

4

李沆奏事

　　李沆是宋真宗时的宰相。每次上朝，他总要将各种坏消息上奏给皇帝知道，如全国各地的犯罪率、社会道德的败坏、自然灾害等等。皇帝听了很不高兴，脸色都变了。

　　李沆的同僚说："为什么你老向皇上报告坏事呢？我们这些人有幸在天下太平的时候做官。你奏的这些事都有有关部门经管，有必要向皇上启奏，让他不高兴吗？就是要上奏，也最好等事情过去之后，再告诉皇上。"

　　李沆说："我不同意。我就是要让皇上心里有事忧虑。如果他不知忧虑，就会放纵自己，无所不为了。"

点评： 一个人有忧患意识，就能防止自满情绪的产生。

5

SYMPTOMS

Bian Que was a famous physician in the 5th century B.C. One day he happened to meet Duke Huan of Cai.

"I believe Your Highness is suffering from some disease," he said to the duke after observing him for a while. "The affected area is between the skin and the muscles."

"But I'm fine," said the duke.

"If you do not cure it, it can get worse," Bian Que warned the duke before he left.

The duke dismissed his warning. "A doctor always tries to find something wrong with a healthy man just to show off."

Ten days later Bian Que met him again.

"Your disease is getting into the muscles," he warned the duke. "It'll get worse if it is not treated."

The duke was not pleased. He ignored the warning.

Another ten days went by before Bian Que saw the duke.

"Your disease has gone into the intestines. You need urgent treatment."

The duke turned the physician away with a sullen face.

Ten days later Bian Que saw the duke again. But he walked away without a word. Seeing him act oddly, the duke sent an aide to query him.

"When the duke's disease was between the skin and the

5

讳疾忌医

扁鹊是公元前五世纪的名医。有一天他见到蔡桓公。他观察了蔡桓公一会儿，说："我看，大王有病，病在皮肤浅表部位。"

蔡桓公说："我身体很好，没有病。"

扁鹊说："大王的病如果不医治，会重起来。"

蔡桓公不听。扁鹊走后，蔡桓公说："做医生的总想在好端端的人身上找出毛病来，以显示自己医术高明。"

过了十天，扁鹊又来见桓公。

他说："大王的病已经到肌肉里了，如不医治，将会更重。"

桓公听了很不高兴，没有理睬他。

又过了十天，扁鹊又遇见桓公。

"大王的病已进入肠胃，需要急诊。"

蔡桓公沉下脸来，将扁鹊打发走了。

再过了十天，扁鹊看到桓公，一言不发，回头就走。

桓公很奇怪，就派人去问他。

扁鹊说："病在皮肤浅表部位，敷药就可以治好；病进入肌肉，针灸也有疗效；病到了肠胃，还可以用火

muscles," said Bian Que, "it can be treated easily with some ointment. When it got into the muscles, acupuncture could be applied. When it invaded the intestines, a mixture of herbal medicine could still be effective. But by the time it has sunk into the bone marrow, there is no cure. His disease has reached its terminal stage. I cannot recommend any more treatment. It's too late."

Five days later, the duke felt pain all over his body. He immediately sent for Dr. Bian Que, but the physician had already left the country. Shortly afterwards, the duke died.

COMMENT: Small changes can lead to a big change; difference of degrees can lead to difference in kind. This is the case in the natural world as well as in the human society.

煎汤来治疗；如今病已入骨髓，我就毫无办法了。现在大王的病已到了末期，无药可救了。"

五天后，桓公周身疼痛，急忙派人找扁鹊医生。但扁鹊已经离开蔡国。不久，蔡桓公就病死了。

点评：小变引起大变，量变引起质变，此理自然界和人类社会皆通。

人
rén
man; human

原来的"人"字有头、有手、有脚。后来此字简化成只有两只脚，但依然看上去像一个人。
The pictograph of a man. Originally it had head, hands and legs. Now only the legs are kept but it still looks like a man.

6

THE GENERAL'S CONCERN

The king of Qin decided to invade Chu. He asked a young general named Li Xin, "If I appoint you as commander-in-chief, how many men do you need?"

"Two hundred thousand should be sufficient."

The king then asked General Wang Jian, a veteran army commander, how many men he would need.

"I can't do with fewer than six hundred thousand."

"You are too timid," the king said. "I'll let General Li Xin lead the expedition."

General Li Xin's army was defeated by the overwhelming force of Chu. When he came back, the king fired him. Then the king called on General Wang Jian.

"I should have listened to you," he said apologetically. "Now Chu's army is on the border. Please help me."

Wang Jian declined. "I'm too old. I can't live up to your expectations. Please find somebody else."

The king apologized again. Wang Jian agreed to come out. "But I must have six hundred thousand men."

"Whatever you say, my general," said the king.

Wang Jian was appointed commander-in-chief of the Qin army. On the day of his departure for the front, the king saw him off to the outskirts of the capital.

6

将军求封地

　　秦王打算攻打楚国。他问年轻的大将李信："如果你做统帅，要多少人马？"

　　李信说："二十万足够了。"

　　秦王又问老将军王翦。

　　"我非六十万不可。"

　　秦王说："年纪大的人到底胆子小，我让李信带兵。"

　　李信的大军被楚军以压倒性的优势打败。回国后，秦王把李信革职，亲自去见王翦。

　　"我后悔没有听你的话，现在楚军已到边境，请将军辛苦一趟吧。"

　　王翦推辞说："我已经老了，不能为主公效劳，主公还是另派别人去吧。"

　　秦王直向他赔不是，王翦只好同意出马。

　　他说："那么，我非要六十万人马不可。"

　　秦王说："就照将军说的办。"

　　秦王拜王翦为大将。出兵的那天，他亲自把王翦送到秦都的郊外。

　　王翦说："我有一点事请求主公。请主公赏给我一

"I have a request," said Wang Jian. "Could Your Majesty give me some good estate?"

"Of course," said the king. "You won't be poor."

"Well, many meritorious officers did not get their due. I thought I should take this opportunity to ask some favor for the sake of my children."

The king laughed and reassured him.

On his way to the battle front, General Wang Jian wrote to the king repeating his request.

"Aren't you overdoing it?" asked his deputy.

"Not at all," said General Wang Jian. "The king is a suspicious man. He put me in charge of the entire army. If I don't ask him for farmland and houses, if I don't let him know I'm thinking of these things, he may suspect me of having my own agenda. I want to put his mind at ease so that he will trust me and give me a free hand in the battlefield."

"You are very thoughtful."

At the front, General Wang Jian fortified his defense but refused to engage the enemy despite repeated challenges. He fed his troops with good food and let them spend time training and playing sports.

For nearly a year, all was quiet on the front. The commander of the Chu army concluded that Qin's army was to strengthen its defense, not to attack Chu. So he decided to pull back his troops.

While his men were withdrawing, General Wang Jian launched a surprise offensive. The Qin army dealt a crushing blow to Chu's forces, capturing a lot of Chu's territory and taking the king of Chu prisoner.

Upon his return, General Wang Jian was awarded a huge

些上好的田产。"

秦王说："当然可以。你不用怕受穷。"

王翦说："许多过去有功劳的将领都没有得到应得的俸禄，所以我要乘现在这个机会，为晚辈留点产业。"

秦王大笑起来，完全答应了王翦。

在去前线的路上，王翦不断地写信给秦王请求赏赐。

他的副将问他："将军这样做，是不是有点过头了？"

王翦回答说："一点也没有。主公对人一向不信任。现在他把全国的精兵都交给我。如果我不多多要求田产，不让他知道我牵挂的只是这点小事，他会疑心我的。我让他安心，他就会放手让我指挥作战。"

55

副将说："将军确实高明。"

王翦到了前线，叫将士们坚壁而守，任凭敌人挑战，始终不应战。将士们酒足饭饱之余，王翦让他们操练身体，做运动。这样过了一年，没有和楚军交手。楚军的统帅于是认为秦军的目的是加强驻防，不是攻打楚国，就下令退兵。

没想到楚军正在后退的时候，王翦挥军追杀，重创楚军，占领了大片楚国疆土，最后将楚王俘虏。

amount of gold. Then he retired.

COMMENT: Wang Jian understood his king and knew how to communicate with him. Thus he gained his confidence. He understood his enemy and was well-versed in the art of war. With a massive force at his command, it was not surprising that he won victory.

王翦凯旋归来，得到秦王的重金赏赐后，就告老还乡。

点评：王翦了解秦王，知道如何与他沟通，因此博得了秦王的信任。王翦又了解敌人，熟谙兵法，由他统帅一支大军，难怪会打胜仗。

立
lì
stand

此字上部画的是人，下部的一画代表地面，即人站在地上之意。

The pictograph portrays a man standing, the upper part representing a man with arms and legs stretching out, beneath him a horizontal line meaning the ground.

7

ARMY ETIQUETTE

In 158 B.C., the Huns invaded the northern border of China. To strengthen the border defense, Emperor Wen of the Han dynasty appointed Generals Liu Li, Xu Li and Zhou Yafu to three garrisons respectively.

Once the emperor paid a visit to these garrisons. His party was able to go straight into the barracks of Generals Liu Li and Xu Li. The generals and soldiers came out on horseback to greet him and see him off. When the royal entourage reached General Zhou's barracks, however, it was stopped at the entrance by armed soldiers. The emperor's vanguard announced that the emperor was coming. But the officer replied, "We only take orders from General Zhou."

Soon the emperor arrived, but his entourage was not permitted to proceed. A messenger was sent to General Zhou with royal credentials to inform him of the emperor's arrival. Thereupon the general ordered the gate of the barracks to be thrown open.

"Galloping is not allowed." the guards told the royal carriage drivers. The royal entourage moved slowly inside. General Zhou, together with his officers, waited in full uniform.

"Forgive me for not kneeling, Your Majesty," said the general as he bowed to the emperor. "A soldier in armor only salutes in the military manner."

7

军　纪

公元前 158 年，匈奴侵犯中国北方的边境。为了巩固边防，汉文帝任命刘礼、徐厉和周亚夫三员大将驻军边境地区。

有一次皇上去边境视察军队。到了刘礼和徐厉的军营，他的车马可以一路进去，驻防将军和士兵骑着马，迎送皇上。可是到了周亚夫将军的军营，却被拦在军营门口不准入内。皇帝的前锋对守军说皇上要来了。可是把守军营的武官说："我们只听从周将军的命令。"

过了一会儿，汉文帝到了，但不准进入。汉文帝于是派使者拿着天子的符节，通知周亚夫皇上驾到。周亚夫这才下令打开军营大门。

把守营门的官兵告诉天子的马车夫说："军营内车马不准奔驰。"皇帝一行就放慢步伐，进入军营。周亚夫身着军装，率领将官，等候皇上。

周亚夫向皇上行礼说："我身着盔甲不能跪拜，只能以军礼向皇上致敬。请皇上原谅。"

皇上挺直身体，向军队致礼。视察结束后，他派人向周亚夫将军表示谢意。

The emperor straightened up and saluted the army. At the end of his inspection, he sent a messenger to General Zhou to thank him for his trouble.

"Now there is a real general," the emperor said to the officials of the royal entourage as he was leaving. "The other two garrisons are like child's play. No discipline. No rule. They could be taken prisoner if the enemy stages a surprise attack. But with General Zhou Yafu, you cannot take a chance."

He went on praising General Zhou for a long time. Soon the general was promoted to be the commander-in-chief for the defense of the capital.

60

COMMENT: If you bend the rules to please your boss, you often lose more than you gain.

軍　纪

　　皇上离开周亚夫的军营后，对随行人员说："这才是一位真正的将军。其他两个军营军纪散漫，没有威仪，如同儿戏。敌人如果来袭击，很可能当俘虏。但是到了周亚夫的军营，谁敢冒险？"

　　皇上一路上对周亚夫赞不绝口。不久，周亚夫被提升为中尉，掌管京师兵权。

点评：如果你罔顾规章制度来曲意取悦上司，你失去的往往比得到的更多。

61

大
dà
big; great

此字像一个手脚伸开的人，表示"大"的概念。
The pictograph of a man stretching his arms and legs to the limit. It conveys the idea of being big.

8

FORESTALLMENT

Gan Mao was prime minister of Qin. One day one of his subordinates overheard the king talking to Gongsun Yan.

"I am going to name you prime minister," the king said.

The next day Gan Mao went to see the king and offered his congratulations. "Your Majesty has selected an excellent candidate as my replacement."

"Who is going to be your replacement?" The king was surprised.

"I heard you are going to appoint Gongsun Yan to be my successor."

"Who told you so?"

"Gongsun Yan himself."

The king was so annoyed he sent Gongsun Yan into exile on account of having disclosed a confidential matter.

COMMENT: Leaks spoil then as they spoil today.

8

甘茂相秦

　　甘茂是秦国的宰相。有一天，他的下属听见国王对公孙衍说："寡人想要任命贤卿为宰相。"

　　第二天，甘茂去见国王，向他道喜："恭喜大王已经获得一位贤相来代替臣。"

　　国王听了很惊奇，"谁会代替你？"

　　"我听说大王准备任命公孙衍为宰相。"

　　"谁告诉你的？"

　　"是公孙衍告诉臣的。"

　　国王听了很生气，认为公孙衍泄露了朝廷机密，就把他赶出朝廷。

点评：泄密在古代和今天都一样会坏事。

9

MEASURE FOR MEASURE

Yuan Ang was a minister under Emperor Wen of the Han dynasty. He was honest and outspoken, but was often vilified by Eunuch Zhao Tan who, thanks to his knowledge of astrology, had found favor with the emperor. Yuan Ang was upset.

"You need to humiliate the eunuch in public," his nephew suggested. "Then the emperor will stop listening to his slanders."

One day the emperor was going out and Eunuch Zhao Tan was seated by his side in the royal carriage. Yuan Ang came across them at the gate of the palace.

"It's a great honor to ride with Your Majesty," he said. "Only those who have outstanding merits and abilities should be given such honor. But we don't have many such people. I wonder why Your Majesty allows a eunuch to sit by your side."

Emperor Wen chuckled and ordered Eunuch Zhao Tan to get off his carriage. The latter was so humiliated he was on the edge of tears. Since then no matter how he bad-mouthed Yuan Ang, the emperor turned a deaf ear to his words.

COMMENT: The best way to neutralize your opponent is to undermine his credibility.

9

以牙还牙

袁盎是汉文帝手下的一位大臣。他为人正派，说话直率，但常常遭到宦官赵谈的诽谤。赵谈因为善于星术，受到皇帝宠幸。袁盎深以为苦。

袁盎的侄子对他说："你必须在大庭广众之下羞辱这个太监。这样一来，皇上就不会再相信他的诽谤了。"

有一天，皇帝出宫，赵谈同车陪同。袁盎在宫门口遇见他们。

他对皇帝说："跟天子共乘马车是很光荣的。只有天下的英才豪杰才能享受这样的光荣。但是，如今本朝这种人才不多。我不知道为什么陛下要让一名太监同车。"

汉文帝笑了笑，就命令赵谈下车。赵谈被羞辱得几乎哭了出来。从此以后，无论他怎样说袁盎的坏话，皇帝都不听了。

点评：使对手失去影响力的最好方式是破坏他的信誉。

10

BORROWED AUTHORITY

A tiger caught a fox and was about to eat it.

"Don't you dare eat me!" said the fox. "I am sent by God to be the king of the jungle. If you do me any harm, you'll run afoul with God."

"What proof do you have that you are sent by God?" demanded the tiger.

"Follow me and you'll witness how other animals react when they see me."

The tiger agreed and walked behind the fox. When other animals saw them, they shied away. The tiger was convinced that they were afraid of the fox.

COMMENT: Self-promotion, when done foxily, can be quite effective.

10

狐假虎威

老虎抓住了一只狐狸要吃它。

狐狸说："你敢吃我？我是天帝派到森林里来做兽王的。你如果伤害我，就是违抗天帝的命令。"

老虎说："你有什么证据说是天帝派你来的？"

狐狸说："跟我来，你看百兽怕不怕我？"

老虎同意了。它跟着狐狸一路走去。森林中的野兽看见它们，都吓走了。老虎于是相信了狐狸，以为百兽的确怕狐狸。

点评：借他人之力提高自己的形象，如果做得巧妙，会相当有效。

11

THREE ARTISTS

There was a king whose right eye was blind and right leg crippled. One day he had an artist draw a portrait for him. The artist portrayed the king as a mighty warrior. His eyes were bright and piercing and his legs muscular like an athlete's. The king was not happy about the painting.

"You are just a sycophant. This is not me." He ordered the guards to take the artist away and throw him into prison.

A second artist was summoned. Upon learning what had happened before, the artist drew a picture of the king exactly the way he looked. The king was not pleased at all.

"What art is it?" he questioned the artist angrily and had him imprisoned, too.

The third artist came. He looked at the king up close and from a distance to choose the perfect viewpoint. The king appeared in a hunting outfit in his portrait. He was shooting an arrow on horseback with the right leg hidden from view. Only his left eye was open as he was taking aim at a fox in the distance.

The king was satisfied. He awarded the artist a bag of gold and praised him as the number one artist in the country.

COMMENT: Flattery is the art of telling a man exactly what he thinks of himself. As a management tool, flattery is indispensable in business and political life: praising superiors so that they will be well-disposed toward you; praising inferiors so that they will be more cooperative. But it should be used with discretion. Flattery has many forms. Ignoring someone's imperfection is one; minimizing his failings is another. Doing it subtly is essential to success.

三个画家

从前有一个国王，他的右眼是瞎的，右腿是瘸的。他召来一个画家为他画像。这个画家把国王画得很英武，双目炯炯有神，两腿粗壮有力。

国王看过画后，气愤地说："你是个马屁精，这不像我。"他叫卫兵把这个画家带出去，投入监牢。

国王又召来一个画家。这个画家了解到第一个画家的遭遇后，就把国王画得很逼真。

国王看过画像后，怒气冲冲地说："这叫什么艺术？"这个画家也被投入了监牢。

第三个画家来了后，仔细地从近处和远处观察了国王。他的画里，国王在打猎。国王手举弓箭，骑在马上，正好遮住了那条瘸腿。只有左眼睁开，瞄准前方的一只狐狸。

国王看了十分高兴，奖给他一袋金子，并称他为"国内第一画师"。

点评：奉承作为一种管理工具，无论是从政或是经商，都必不可少。奉承上级，他对你就会有好感；奉承下级，他们就会更加合作。奉承的方式有多种多样。有的是忽略一个人的不足，有的是缩小一个人的缺点。但要做得巧妙才能奏效。

12

ONE HUNDRED HONEYED PHRASES

After passing the imperial examination in Beijing, a young man was appointed to a position in a provincial city. He went to bid good-bye to his mentor, a senior government minister.

"It's not easy to make a career in provincial places. You must be careful."

"Don't worry, sir," the young man said. "I've prepared a hundred honeyed phrases. When I meet an official, I'll use one on him. He'll surely be pleased."

His mentor gave him a disapproving look. "How can you do that? You are a gentleman. You should not stoop to flattery."

"Unfortunately most people like flattery," said the student, looking helpless. "Only very few true gentlemen like you don't like it."

"I agree." His mentor nodded with a smile.

Later the young man related the story to a friend of his. "I've just used one item in my stock. Now I have ninety-nine honeyed sayings left."

COMMENT: Everybody likes flattery including you.

12

高 帽 子

有个门生通过科举考试以后，出京去做地方官。他先到他的老师——一个大官那里去告别。

老师对门生说："出外做官，很不容易，千万要小心谨慎。"

门生回答："请老师放心。门生已经预备好一百顶高帽子，每人送一顶，管叫地方上人人高兴。"

老师听了很不高兴。"你是正人君子，怎么可以这样呢？"

门生装出无可奈何的样子说："天下不喜欢戴高帽子的实在太少了。像老师这样的君子能有几个呢？"

老师听了点点头说："你说得不错。"

门生出来对朋友说："我的一百顶高帽子，现在只剩下九十九顶了。"

点评：谁都喜欢奉承，你也不例外。

13

A WORD OF ADVICE MAKES A WORLD OF DIFFERENCE

Daoguang was the sixth emperor of the Qing dynasty. His first three sons all died young. His fourth son, Yi Zhu, naturally became the heir apparent according to the imperial tradition. But the emperor's favorite was Yi Xin, his sixth son.

Yi Zhu's mentor, Du Shoutian, was a learned man with a calculating mind. Concerned by the emperor's attitude, he was anxious for a chance to help his pupil.

One day Emperor Daoguang took the princes on a hunting expedition. Before their departure, Du said to Yi Zhu, "When you are in the hunting ground, do not kill. You must also forbid your subordinates to kill anything."

"What should I say if my father asks me?"

Du told Yi Zhu what to say.

The princes were eager to show off their hunting skills, especially Yi Xin who managed to catch the biggest quarry. But Yi Zhu did nothing. He just sat on his horse, looking on.

At the end of the day, the emperor was not pleased at all to see Yi Zhu going home empty-handed. "You are here all day but you did not even catch a rabbit."

"I chose not, Father," Yi Zhu was ready to seize the opportunity. "If I ordered my men to hunt, I would have caught quite a few animals. But it is spring time, the time when

13

皇帝的师傅

道光帝是清朝的第六个皇帝。他的三个儿子，老大、老二、老三，未成年就死了。第四子奕詝按礼制是当然的大阿哥。可是道光帝宠爱第六子奕䜣。

奕詝的老师杜受田是个学问渊博又富于心计的人。他很为道光帝的摇摆不定而担忧，时刻寻找机会帮助奕詝。

一天，道光帝要带领诸王子到南苑狩猎。临行前，杜受田对奕詝说："殿下在南苑只能观看，不能动手，并且还得约束你的侍卫也不得捕杀。"

奕詝不懂，问道："要是父王责问怎么办？"

杜受田告诉奕詝应如何作答。

王子们兴高采烈地挽弓发弩，争先恐后要在父王面前作一番表现。特别是奕䜣猎物最多，而奕詝却始终坐在马上不动。

围猎结束后，只有奕詝一无所获。道光帝很不高兴，就质问他："你校猎一整天，怎么连一只兔子都没有打到？"

奕詝回答道："儿臣是故意不打的。如果儿臣指挥麾下侍卫动手，当然能够打到一些鸟兽。只是儿臣想到

animals are mating and reproducing. I don't have the heart to kill. Moreover, I'm not interested in competing with my younger brothers."

"Absolutely." The emperor was greatly impressed. Convinced that his fourth son possessed the requisite qualities for being a ruler, he soon announced that Yi Zhu was to be his successor.

COMMENT: Sometimes doing nothing is the best course of action.

眼下正值春回大地，鸟兽生长繁殖之际，儿臣实在不忍心杀害生灵。再说，我做兄长的也不愿和弟弟争高低啊。"

道光帝听了，极为高兴，连声称赞："对！对！"

奕詝的话使道光帝相信他具备做帝王的品德。不久他就宣布立奕詝为大阿哥。

点评：有时候最佳的行动方案是不做任何事。

众
zhòng
crowd; many

三个人表示一群。
Three people together conveys the idea of a crowd.

14

A WILY RABBIT

Lord Mengchang was prime minister of Qi. Like many aristocrats of his day, he kept a large number of lodger-guests—men from all walks of life, scholars, soldiers, knights-errant, even refugees—who sought fortune under the roofs of a nobleman.

Lord Mengchang treated them generously. When he talked with a lodger-guest, his secretary would sit behind the screen to take notes. After the guest was gone, gifts would be sent to those whose names had been mentioned by the guest. One of his guests was Feng Huan.

Sword Song

When Feng Huan was introduced to him, Lord Mengchang asked, "What are your interests?"

"Nothing special."

"What can you do?"

"Nothing particular."

Lord Mengchang was amused by his answers.

"All right. Be my guest anyway."

He had the man put in the hostel for newcomers. There the guests had only vegetables for meal. A few days later, Lord

14

狡兔三窟

　　孟尝君是齐国的相国，他家财万贯，又热情好客，天下豪杰之士都慕名而来。许多人在拜访他以后，就在他家常住下来，成为门客。其中有读书人、军人、游侠，乃至流民。孟尝君对待门客慷慨大方。他接见门客时，屏风后面有一位秘书记笔记。客人离开后，孟尝君就派人到客人提起过的人那里送礼问候。

　　冯谖是孟尝君的一个门客。

剑　　歌

　　冯谖来投奔孟尝君时，孟尝君问他："你有什么爱好？"

　　冯谖说："我没有什么特别的爱好。"

　　"你有什么本事？"

　　"我什么本事也没有。"

　　孟尝君笑了笑说："那你就先住下吧。"

　　他把冯谖安排在新来的门客住的馆舍，那里的门客只吃粗茶淡饭。

Mengchang asked the warden of the guest house how Feng Huan was doing.

"He likes to beat his sword and sing to himself: 'Sword, Sword, let us go home. I have no fish for my meals.'"

Lord Mengchang moved Feng Huan to a better hostel where fish was served. A few days later, he asked the warden about Feng Huan.

"He likes to beat his sword and sing to himself: 'Sword, Sword, let us go home. I have no carriage to ride in.'"

Lord Mengchang transferred Feng Huan to a hostel for distinguished guests and provided a carriage for him. A few days later he asked the warden about Feng Huan.

"He still beats his sword but this time he is singing: 'Sword, Sword, let us go home. I have to provide for my family.'"

His fellow guests were put off. The man seemed insatiable. But Lord Mengchang did not seem to mind. "Does he have a family?" he asked.

"His mother."

Lord Mengchang had food and clothing sent to his mother regularly. Thereafter Feng Huan stopped complaining.

Burning the Books

Lord Mengchang had three thousand lodger-guests. The income from his fief in Xue was not enough to meet his expenditure, and so he supplemented it with interest on the loan he made to the people in Xue.

One year his debtors were unable to make payment because they had a poor harvest. Lord Mengchang put up a

几天后，孟尝君问管事的冯骥怎么样。

管事的回答："他喜欢一边敲着他的剑，一边唱：'剑啊，剑啊，咱们回去吧，这儿吃饭没有鱼。'"

孟尝君就让冯骥搬到好一些的馆舍去住，那里可以吃到鱼。过了几天，孟尝君问管事的冯骥在干些什么。

"他还是喜欢敲着那把剑，边敲边唱：'剑啊，剑啊，咱们回去吧，这儿出门没有车。'"

孟尝君就让冯骥搬到贵宾住的馆舍，还给他备了一套车马。没过多久，孟尝君又问管事冯骥的情况。

"他还是边敲剑边唱歌。这次唱的是：'剑啊，剑啊，咱们回去吧，我没有钱养家。'"

别的门客都讨厌冯骥，觉得这个人不知足。孟尝君却不在乎，他问管事："此人有家眷吗？"

"他有个母亲。"

孟尝君就经常派人给冯骥的老母送吃送穿。冯骥这才不敲剑不唱歌了。

烧 账 簿

孟尝君有三千个门客。他从封地薛城得到的收入不够开销，所以还要用他在薛城放债的利息来贴补。

有一年收成不好，债户无法按时付款。孟尝君就贴

notice seeking someone who understood accounting to go to his fief to collect money. Feng Huan offered to go.

"Who is this man?" Lord Mengchang asked the warden, having already forgotten him.

"The man used to tap his sword and sing his complaints."

"Aha, Mr. Feng is going to do something for me after all," Lord Mengchang chuckled.

"Is there anything Your Highness wants me to buy?" Feng Huan asked.

"Buy whatever you think I need in my house."

After arriving in Xue, Feng Huan collected some debt and then hosted a party to which all the debtors were invited. He asked everybody to bring their loan documents along. Feng Huan talked with each of them to determine his financial status. If a man could repay, a schedule would be worked out. If not, Feng Huan would burn the loan documents. Then he spoke to the gathering of debtors.

"Lord Mengchang lent you money to help you with your business. For those who can pay, we've worked out a schedule. For those who can't, the debt is cancelled and the money you borrowed will be Lord Mengchang's gift."

The debtors rose to their feet and gave him a standing ovation.

Lord Mengchang was furious after hearing Feng Huan's briefing. "What have you done? How could you burn the loan documents? And you even threw a party for those who owe me money?"

"If I did not hold a party, I wouldn't have gathered all the debtors. For those who can repay, I've worked out a schedule. For those who can't, there is no point pressing them.

了一张通告，要找一个懂会计的门客去薛城讨债。冯骓自告奋勇前往薛城。

孟尝君问管事："这个人是谁？"原来他已经把冯骓忘了。

"他就是从前那个弹剑唱歌的人。"

孟尝君笑了笑说："啊，冯先生要为我做点事了。"

冯骓问道："主公要我买点什么回来？"

"你看我家缺什么，就买什么吧。"

冯骓到了薛城，讨到一些债后，就办了一席酒，邀请所有的债户来喝酒。他要每个人把账簿带来。冯骓同债户们一一交谈，问明了情况。凡是能还债的，就约好归还的期限；凡是还不起的，冯骓就把他们的账簿收回，一把火给烧了。

然后，他对大家说："孟尝君借钱给你们是为了帮助你们做生意。还得起的，我们已经约定了归还的期限。还不起的，账簿都烧掉了，你借的钱就是孟尝君送给你的。"

这番话说得大家鼓掌叫好，称谢不已。

孟尝君听了冯骓的汇报，不由得火冒三丈。他气呼呼地责备冯骓："你搞的什么名堂？你怎么能把账簿烧掉呢？你居然还摆酒席请欠债的吃？"

冯骓回答说："我不办酒席，怎么能把债户全都招来呢？现在付得起的，已经约好期限还债。付不起的，

If you press them too hard, they would run away. Forgiving uncollectible debts will win you the heart and mind of the people. You told me to buy whatever you need in your house. You've got plenty of valuables in your house. You have fine dogs and horses, and there is no shortage of pretty women. I figured what you need is loyalty from your people. Xue is your fief. You should take care of the people there, not exploit them like a merchant. I cancelled the debt in your name, burned the documents in your name. The people of Xue cheered you."

But Lord Mengchang was not pleased.

Three Burrows

A year later, Lord Mengchang lost his post because the king suspected him of disloyalty. As he returned to his fief in Xue, the residents, old and young, men and women, came out to greet him. Lord Mengchang's heart was filled with warmth.

"So this is the loyalty you've bought for me," he said to Feng Huan, thankfully.

"A wily rabbit needs three burrows to survive," said Feng Huan. "You've got only one. Let me go to the State of Liang and I'll make the king of Qi restore your position."

He knew King Hui of Liang had always admired Lord Mengchang and wanted to engage him as prime minister.

"Lord Mengchang is out of office," Feng Huan told King Hui of Liang. "As you know, Qi became a superpower under his management. But the king of Qi heard some rumors and dismissed him. If Lord Mengchang comes to work for you, his knowledge and experience would be very useful."

逼也没用。逼急了，他索性跑到别的地方去。免掉那些收不回来的债，会使百姓对你感恩戴德。你嘱咐我拣你家缺少的东西买回来。我看你家金银财宝、骏马、好狗、美女，什么都不缺。唯独缺少的，就是百姓对你的忠心。薛城是你的封地，你应当爱护那里的百姓，而不应该像商人那样盘剥他们。我免除了他们的债，烧掉了借契，说是你赏给他们的。老百姓都向你欢呼。"

孟尝君听了老大不高兴。

狡兔三窟

过了一年，齐王听信谣言，怀疑孟尝君不忠，免去了他相国的职务。孟尝君回到自己的封地时，只见人们扶老携幼，前来迎接他。孟尝君心里充满了温暖。他感激地对冯谖说："这就是先生给我买下的情义啊。"

冯谖说："一只狡猾的兔子要有三个洞穴才能安身。现在您只有一个洞穴。让我上梁国去一趟，我一定能叫齐王重新用您。"

冯谖知道梁王向来钦佩孟尝君，早就想聘他当相国。

冯谖对梁王说："孟尝君不做官了。大王知道，齐国能够强大，全是孟尝君治理得好。现在齐王听信谣言，辞退了他。如果孟尝君来投奔大王，他的知识和经验一

King Hui dispatched an envoy to Qi with 10,000 ounces of gold as gift and an invitation to Lord Mengchang, but the lord accepted neither at Feng Huan's advice. Three times the envoy of Liang called upon him. Three times Lord Mengchang declined King Hui's invitation.

The king of Qi was troubled at the news. He hastened to offer his apology to Lord Mengchang and restore him to office. He also added a thousand households to the lord's fief and gave him 10,000 ounces of gold as bonus.

"You've got two burrows now," Feng Huan said to Lord Mengchang. "Let's make a third one."

At his suggestion, Lord Mengchang asked the king to move the royal ancestral temple to his fief in Xue. This would make Xue a sacred place. No matter what happened, the king of Qi could not attack Xue. And if Xue was attacked, the king would be compelled to come to his rescue.

When the construction of the royal temple was completed, Feng Huan said, "Now Your Highness has three burrows. You should feel secure now."

Forgive and Forget

As Lord Mengchang resumed his office, those who had left him came back one by one.

"I had treated them well," Lord Mengchang complained to Feng Huan. "But when I was stripped of my office, they left me without a qualm. What face they've got to come back? I feel like spitting in their faces!"

Feng Huan bowed to him.

定对大王有用。"

梁王派遣使者带了黄金一万两前往聘请孟尝君。孟尝君听从冯骢的意见，没有同意。梁国的使者往返了三次，孟尝君总是推辞。

齐王知道后，五内不安，连忙向孟尝君道歉，让他官复原职，还送给他黄金一万两，又给他的封地薛城加了一千户人家。

冯骢说："现在您有两个洞穴了。我们还要挖第三个。"

冯骢建议孟尝君请齐王把先王的宗庙搬到薛城。这样一来，薛城就成为一块神圣之地。不管发生什么，齐王绝不会攻打薛城。而且，假如别人攻打薛城，齐王将不得不派兵援救。

先王的宗庙在薛城造好后，冯骢对孟尝君说："主公的三个洞穴都齐备了。现在您可以高枕无忧了。"

不 记 怨

那些走掉的门客听说孟尝君重新当上了相国，一个一个又回来投奔他。

孟尝君很恼火，对冯骢说："我待他们算是不错。可是当我失势的时候，他们都溜了，一点都不觉得不好意思。现在他们有什么脸来见我？如果有谁来见我，

"Are you apologizing on their behalf?" Lord Mengchang asked.

"No. I was apologizing for what you just said."

"Explain."

"In this world," replied Feng Huan. "The rich and powerful have many friends and the poor and weak have few. This is not going to change. Have you noticed the shoppers in the marketplace? In the morning they push and jostle their way into the marketplace. But when it gets dark, they turn away from the place without looking back. Not that they like it less in the evening than they do in the morning, but what they want is not there in the evening. When you lost your position, your guests went away for the same reason—they couldn't get what they wanted. There is no need to bear grudge against them. I hope you will treat them exactly as you did before."

Lord Mengchang took Feng Huan's advice and had the names of the five hundred men blacklisted scraped from his record.

COMMENT: "A wily rabbit always has three burrows" is an immortal saying of Feng Huan. His idea was that one should prepare for bad times while fortune was smiling on him and keep a following of grateful people in case one should need them. His advice stood Lord Mengchang in good stead. The lord managed to keep his position as prime minister of Qi for many years despite the chaos, trickery and treachery around him. Feng Huan's burning of loan books reminds me of the parable of the shrewd manager for a rich man in *Luke*. Jesus used the fable to exhort his followers to use worldly wealth to gain friends, so that when it was gone, they would be welcome into eternal dwellings.

我就唾他的脸。"

冯骓听罢向孟尝君鞠了一躬。

"你是代门客们向我道歉？"

"不是的，我是为你刚才的失言道歉啊。"

孟尝君说："我不懂你的意思。"

冯骓回答道："在这个世界上，富贵的人有很多朋友；贫贱的人朋友很少。这是改变不了的。您难道没有见过赶集的人群吗？天一亮，大伙儿你推我挤进入集市。可是到了晚上，他们离开集市，头也不回。这并不是他们喜欢早晨，讨厌黄昏，而是到了晚上，集市上没有他们想要的东西。当您失去高位时，门客出走，原因是一样的，因为他们在您这里得不到想要的东西。您不能赌气，还是要像当初一样，好好招待他们。"

孟尝君接受了冯骓的意见，就把原来已上了黑名单的五百个门客的名字统统抹掉了。

点评："狡兔三窟"是冯骓的不朽名言。冯骓认为，一个人得意的时候，要为失意的时候未雨绸缪，要善待他人以便日后有用。多亏他的谋略见识，孟尝君才得以在尔虞我诈、动荡不安的政局中保住官位，做了多年的相国。冯骓烧掉账簿的举动，使我想起《路加福音》中的一个财主的管家减少债户债务的寓言。耶稣用这个寓言教导门徒，要用今世的钱财结交朋友。这样，钱财完了的时候，他们就可以被接到永久的家乡居住。

PART III

MANAGING SUBORDINATES

管理下属

1

A RIBBON-RIPPING BANQUET

King Zhuang of Chu was giving a banquet for his ministers and generals. Music was played and toasts were exchanged amid a convivial atmosphere. The banquet went from afternoon into evening and candles were lit. The king asked his concubine, the beautiful Princess Xu, to walk around the hall and pour wine for each guest at the table.

In the midst of laughter and tinkling of glasses, a wind suddenly blew out all the candles, and the banquet hall was enveloped in darkness. Princess Xu happened to stand near a man who, enticed by her beauty, pulled at her clothes until his fingers nearly touched her breast. The princess staved off the intrusion dexterously and ripped the chin ribbon off the man's hat.

She ran up to the king and whispered, "Somebody was trying to pull off my clothes. But I've snatched the chin ribbon off his hat. Please have the candles lit up. I can identify him easily."

Instead of summoning the attendants to light up the candles, the king proposed that everyone take off their hats, loosen their clothes and have a good time. Too willing to oblige, the guests complied right away. When the candles were relit, Princess Xu was unable to identify the man. She was upset.

When the party was over, the king explained to her, "That

1

楚庄王绝缨

一天，楚庄王大宴文武百官。席间美酒佳肴，轻歌曼舞。宴会在欢乐的气氛中从下午进行到黄昏，兴犹未尽。庄王命令点亮蜡烛继续欢宴，还叫他宠爱的许姬向客人轮流敬酒。

正在觥筹交错、笑语不绝之际，忽然吹来一阵风，把所有的蜡烛都吹灭了。宴会厅一片漆黑。有一位官员乘机拉扯许姬的衣服，他的手指几乎触到了许姬的玉胸。

许姬把手一甩，顺势扯断他的帽带，然后匆匆回坐，附耳对楚庄王说："刚才有人拉我的衣服，我扯断了他的帽带。请赶快点亮蜡烛，看谁没有帽带。"

楚庄王没有下令点烛，却大声请众人脱帽解襟，痛痛快快地喝酒。于是大家都把帽子脱下。楚庄王这才叫人重新点亮蜡烛。许姬无法认出刚才企图调戏她的人，很生气。

席散回宫，楚王对她说："酒后失态，人之常情，没有必要大煞风景。这些人忠心耿耿，为我服务。宴会的目的就是要让他们开心。"

三年后，楚国和吴国交战。庄王为吴兵所困，情势

man must've been a little drunk. You needn't make a fuss to spoil the party. These men have worked for me in good faith. I wanted them to have a good time."

Three years went by. War broke out between Chu and its neighbor, Wu. King Zhuang was surrounded by the enemy in a battle, and fought desperately to break out. At this moment, one General Tang rushed to his rescue. The general fought so bravely that the king was able to snatch victory out of defeat.

King Zhuang was filled with gratitude. "I haven't been particularly nice to you, why did you fight so hard to save me?"

He wanted to reward the general, but the general declined his offer.

"Your Majesty, I am the man who harassed Princess Xu at a banquet three years ago. You could have punished me but you overlooked my fault. From that day on I've been looking for a chance to express my gratitude."

COMMENT: The king's handling of the situation was hailed as a quintessential example of being magnanimous to one's subordinates. Such magnanimity is bound to earn their lasting loyalty.

危急。忽然有一位姓唐的将军，杀入重围，救出庄王。
由于他英勇奋战，楚军反败为胜。

楚庄王心怀感激，对他说："我平日对你没有特别
的礼遇，你为什么对我这么忠心？"他要赏赐唐将军，
但将军谢绝了。

他说："我就是三年前那天晚上，对许姬不敬的人。
大王本应处罚我，却忍了下来。从那天起，我一直盼望
有机会报答大王。"

点评：楚庄王的宽宏大量获得了一致好评。一个对下属宽宏大量的人，一定能
赢得他们的忠心。

从
cóng
follow; from

一个人紧紧跟在另一个人后面。后引申为服从、从
等意。
The pictograph shows two men standing close together, one following
the other. It came to mean "obedient" and "from" by extension.

2

BURNING LETTERS

Cao Cao, the ruler of Wei during the Period of the Three Kingdoms, was a man of keen observation and excellent judgment. He was thrifty. His life style was plain. But he shared everything with his subordinates. When it came to rewarding a person with merit, he would not think a thousand ounces of gold as too much. When it came to use of talented men, he would not hesitate to appoint surrendered enemy to be officers in his army.

He was contending with General Yuan Shao for the dominance of northern China. After his forces captured Yuan's stronghold Guandu in modern Henan Province, his advisor discovered secret correspondence between Yuan Shao and many officers in Cao Cao's army who had pledged allegiance to Yuan. The advisor suggested that these officers be arrested and executed for treachery.

Cao Cao thought differently.

"When Yuan Shao was strong, even I was afraid of him. How can I blame others?"

He ordered all the letters be burned and nothing was said of the matter.

At the time Yuan Shao still controlled large areas in the north. Cao Cao understood if he started an investigation, the consequences could be disastrous. Those under investigation

2

曹操焚信

曹操是三国时期魏国的国君。他善于观察人，判断人。他生活节俭，不喜奢华，所有的东西都与部下分享。应当奖赏的人，他不会吝惜千金。降敌中有才能的人，他会毫不犹豫地任用。

他跟另一个军阀袁绍争夺北方。曹军攻下袁绍的据点河南官渡之后，发现了一批曹营里的人暗中向袁绍表忠的书信。曹操的谋士建议严加追究，把写信的人统统抓起来杀掉。曹操不同意。

"袁绍强大的时候我都怕，我怎么能怪别人呢？"

他下令把这些密信付之一炬，一概不去追查。

比	两个人站得很近，仿佛在比身高。
bǐ	The pictograph shows two men standing very close to each other,
compare	facing to the right, as though they were comparing heights.

might mutiny against him. Burning the letters, on the contrary, would demonstrate his magnanimity and reassure those who had secretly corresponded with General Yuan Shao.

In the end Yuan Shao was crushed by him.

COMMENT: Cao Cao knew he could not lead without loyalty. But to command loyalty, he must deserve it, and to expect others to be loyal, he must act as though they were already loyal.

当时，袁绍还占据着北方大片土地。曹操很清楚，如果追查，一定对自己不利。被追查的人会叛逃。相反，烧掉这些信，会安定人心，写信的人会佩服他的宽宏大量。

后来，曹操打败了袁绍。

点评：曹操知道没有部下的忠心就无法率领军队。但是要得到部下的效忠，他必须让部下佩服他。如果希望别人效忠，他就必须表现出好像别人已经对他忠心才行。

97

奔
bēn
run

此字上半部是一个挥臂奔跑的人，下半部是三条腿。
The upper part of this ideograph shows a man running with arms swinging, and the lower part three legs.

3

CUTTING HAIR

Once when his army was passing through a wheat field, Cao Cao issued an order that anyone trampling the crop would be put to death. All the cavalry soldiers got down from their horses to walk. But his own horse ran into the field, causing much damage to the crops. Cao Cao called on his law officer to punish him. But the officer said the army could not be without a commander.

"I laid down the rules," Cao Cao said. "If I were not punished, how could I expect others to follow me?"

He cut off his hair with his sword as a punishment on himself and had it displayed to all his soldiers, symbolizing his head.

COMMENT: A symbol can be a powerful management tool to communicate the culture of the organization and the value of its leadership. Cao Cao used it skillfully to foster the loyalty of his men.

3

曹操割发

有一次，曹军经过麦田，曹操下令士兵不准践踏麦子，否则处死。曹军的骑兵都下马步行。曹操自己的马突然冲进了麦田，损坏了好些麦子。曹操便命令主管官员议罪。但是，主管官员说军队不能没有主帅。

曹操说："我立了法。我不办罪，怎么能统帅下属呢？"

于是，就用剑割下了自己的头发，以象征头颅，将它示众。

点评：用具有象征意义的东西传达一个组织的文化和领导的价值观，不失为一种有效的管理方法。曹操巧妙地运用了它来培养下属的忠心。

4

HUMAN HEAD FOR A LOAN

Cao Cao was engaged in a prolonged campaign, and there was a shortage of food. He asked the commissary what to do. The latter suggested that the food ration be cut by using a smaller measure so that the existing supply could last long enough until new supplies arrived. Cao Cao agreed.

Soon there was much complaint in the army. The soldiers accused Cao Cao of cheating them out of their food. The atmosphere was mutinous. Cao Cao summoned the commissary.

"I want to borrow something from you," he told the man.

"What do you want?"

"Your head."

"But I've done nothing wrong."

"True. But if I don't put you to death, there will be a mutiny. I'll take good care of your family after your death."

The commissary was executed.

Cao Cao told his soldiers, "The man stole grain and used a smaller measure for your food ration. But supplies are coming. Please be patient."

The soldiers accepted his explanation and a potential crisis was averted.

COMMENT: Cao Cao was ruthless, unscrupulous, but good at management, and furthermore, he was endowed with literary talent. This earned him the name of a rogue of many parts. He was at once hated and admired by many Chinese.

4

曹操借头

　　有一次出征，粮食不够。曹操问主管粮食的官员该怎么办。那个官员建议用小斗来量米，以弥补不足，直到下一批粮草运到。曹操同意了。

　　结果，将士们非常不满，说曹操克扣粮食，欺骗大家。军心变得相当不稳。曹操将那个主管粮食的官员召来。

　　"我想向你借一件东西。"

　　"什么东西？"

　　"你的首级。"

　　"但这不是我的过错啊。"

　　"的确不是。但如果我不处死你，军队就会造反。你死后我会好好照顾你的家人的。"

　　曹操处决了这个主管，然后，向将士们宣布："此人用小斗量米，盗窃公粮，所以斩首示众。粮食就要运到了，请大家忍耐一下。"

　　大家接受了他的解释，一场危机才得以避免。

点评：曹操奸诈无情，却擅长管理，又善诗文，是一位多才多艺的奸雄。因此，许多中国人对他又恨又爱。

5

WHEN THE WATER IS TOO CLEAN

One day Emperor Taizong of the Song dynasty received a confidential report that some officials in the government-owned shipping agency were involved in smuggling.

He discussed the matter with his prime minister Lu Mengzheng.

"There are always people who do that sort of thing," he said. "It's impossible to stop them just as it's impossible to fill up the holes in the walls that rats live in. I don't intend to pursue the case. As long as the cargo reaches its destination safe and sound, I would leave them alone if they use their position to do a little smuggling on the side. Only the most serious offenders must be punished. What do you think?"

Lu Mengzheng agreed. "If the water is too clean, there will be no fish. If the ruler is too sharp, he'll have few people willing to work for him. Since we know what they are doing, we can afford to tolerate such people to some extent so that they won't make trouble elsewhere. If we try to get everything right, things may not go as smoothly."

COMMENT: Implicit in their tolerance of wrong-doing is the cost-benefit trade-off of law enforcement. The idea of justice is lofty, but the benefit of enforcing the law must be weighed against the cost of doing so when resources are limited.

5

水至清则无鱼

宋太宗有一次接到一份密奏，说有些负责官船水运的官员假公济私，贩卖私货。

太宗和丞相吕蒙正谈及此事时说："这种事不可能堵得住，就像墙里的鼠穴一样，不可能全部塞住。只要官货能够安全无恙地到达目的地，我看就不必追究了。让他们顺便捎带一些私货贩卖也无妨。只要将情节特别严重的加以处罚，就行了。你说呢？"

吕蒙正表示赞成。"水至清则无鱼，人至察则无徒。我们既然知道他们在干什么，就可以在一定程度上容忍他们，使他们不至于在别处惹是生非。如果我们想把每件事都理顺，事情未必会顺利。"

点评：太宗和吕蒙正之所以容忍犯法，是考虑到执法的成本和效益之间要有个平衡。犯了法要受惩本来不错。但是，当资源有限时，就不得不权衡执法的效益和执法的代价。

6

THE GIFT BOX

Marquis Wen, the ruler of Wei, decided to attack Zhong shan which was ruled by a tyrant. He intended to appoint Yue Yang to be the commander-in-chief.

"Although Yue Yang is a capable, honest man," said his advisor, "his son is an official in Zhongshan. It is better to appoint somebody else."

Marquis Wen asked Yue Yang, "Would that be a problem for you, General?"

"No. I am a man of Wei and I work for the interest of Wei."

When Yue Yang's army reached the border of Zhongshan, his son Yue Shu came to see him on the instructions of the ruler of Zhongshan. Yue Yang rebuked his son for serving a bad ruler but agreed to postpone his attack for a month so that the ruler of Zhongshan could consider submission.

But the ruler of Zhongshan had no intention of doing so. He thought Yue Yang would not attack because of his son. A month later, he sent Yue Shu to Yue Yang's camp again. And again Yue Yang postponed his attack at his son's request. Another month passed, but there was no sign of yielding on the part of Zhongshan. Nevertheless, Yue Yang granted another month's grace when his son came to ask for it.

Back in Wei, many officials were uneasy and questioned his loyalty. But Marquis Wen sent envoys to reassure him and bring

6

礼　盒

中山国国君荒淫无道，魏文侯打算拜乐羊为大将，征伐中山国。

有人反对说："乐羊虽然文武全才，可是他的儿子在中山国做官。最好还是另外指派统帅。"

魏文侯就问乐羊："这会不会成问题？"

乐羊说："这不成问题。我是魏国人，我为魏国效劳。"

乐羊的军队到了中山国边境，中山国国君派他的儿子乐舒来见他。乐羊骂儿子不该服侍一个暴君。不过，他同意给中山国国君一个月期限，让他考虑投降。

可是中山国国君根本不打算投降，他满以为乐羊心疼儿子不至于攻打。一个月过去了，他又叫乐舒去求情，再宽限一个月。乐羊又同意了。又过了一个月，中山国仍然不肯投降。然而，当乐舒来求情时，乐羊又给了一个月的宽限。

魏国朝廷里不少人感到不安，他们怀疑乐羊的忠心。但魏文侯却打发人慰劳乐羊，叫他安心。

乐羊的副将问他："将军，你在等什么呢？"

乐羊说："我在等待时机成熟。"

him gifts.

"What are you waiting for, General?" Yue Yang's deputy asked him.

"I'm waiting for the right moment."

He waited yet another month and then ordered a major offensive. The ruler of Zhongshan killed Yue Shu and had his flesh cut and cooked to make a broth. He had the broth sent to Yue Yang in the hope that it might shock him into retreat. But Yue Yang intensified his attack. Zhongshan's defense collapsed and its ruler committed suicide.

Marquis Wen greeted Yue Yang at the gate of the capital on his return and held a grand party to celebrate his victory. At the end of the banquet, he gave Yue Yang a gift box to take home. Yue Yang expected to find gold and silver inside. But when he opened the box, he found it only contained letters and memorials from those who had expressed their doubts about his loyalty.

He came to realize the great trust Marquis Wen had placed in him. The following day he lost no time in expressing his profound gratitude.

"Without Your Lordship's confidence in me, I could not have won the victory."

"I trusted you because I know what kind of a man you are." Marquis Wen rewarded him a huge estate.

COMMENT: Show your trust to those who work for you, and you will earn their gratitude and loyalty.

一个月后，乐羊下令全线进攻。中山国国君把乐舒杀了，割下他的肉，做成肉羹，给乐羊送去，指望乐羊会难受得神魂颠倒，被迫退兵。可是乐羊加紧攻城。中山国城破，国君自杀。

乐羊得胜回国。魏文侯亲自出城迎接，并在宫中设庆功宴。宴会散后，魏文侯取出一个礼盒，给乐羊带回家。乐羊以为里面装满金银珠宝，可是打开一看，里面装的全是朝廷大臣对他表示怀疑的奏章。

他这才明白魏文侯对他坚定的信任。第二天，他上朝谢恩。

他说："如果没有主公对我的信任，我是不可能打胜仗的。"

魏文侯说："我信任你，因为我知道你的为人。"

他赏给乐羊一大片田产。

点评：你要向那些为你工作的人表示信任，就会赢得他们的感激和忠诚。

7

POWER BANQUET

Shortly after he became the emperor, Taizu, founder of the Song dynasty, invited his comrades-in-arms to a banquet. He was concerned that they might contend with him for power. There were many examples in history in which those who fought shoulder to shoulder to overthrow the old dynasty started killing one another after a new dynasty was established. Taizu wanted to find a way to avoid it.

After much wining and dining, he addressed the banqueters, "Without your help, I could not possibly sit here. But it is not an enviable position to be in. I am uneasy and I don't sleep well. I'd rather be a general than an emperor."

General Shi, who was the highest-ranking army commander, was perplexed.

"What do you mean, Your Majesty?" he asked.

"Which one among you doesn't want to be an emperor?" Taizu said.

"But Your Majesty is mandated by Heaven. Who dare to challenge you?"

"I don't doubt your loyalty," said Taizu, "but what about your subordinates? They may want you to become emperor for their own sake. Even if you have no intention yourself, you might be forced by your subordinates to do something."

The banqueters were alarmed. Their lives would be in

7

杯酒释兵权

宋朝的开国皇帝宋太祖即位后不久，宴请和他一起打下江山的战友们。宋太祖担心这些人会和他争权。一个新王朝建立后，原来并肩作战的人互相残杀，在历史上屡见不鲜。宋太祖希望避免这种局面。

他趁着酒兴对来宾们说："要不是靠你们出力，我绝不会有今天。不过，做天子也实在艰难。如今我忧虑不安，连觉都睡不安稳，还不如做一个将领。"

宋军的最高统帅石将军觉得奇怪，就问宋太祖："陛下还有什么忧虑呢？"

宋太祖说："你们当中，谁不想当皇帝呢？"

"做皇帝是天命，谁敢有不安分的想法？"

宋太祖说："我毫不怀疑你们的一片忠心。但是，你们的部下怎么想呢？他们为自己考虑，会希望你们黄袍加身。你们即使不想做，恐怕也不行。"

众人大吃一惊。如果宋太祖怀疑他们有二心，他们就有性命之虞。

石将军说："我对陛下一片忠心，从来没有想到这点。请陛下指点我们该怎么办。"

danger if they should come under such suspicion.

"I'm loyal to you, Your Majesty," said General Shi. "I've never thought of this before. Please tell us what we should do."

"Life is short. We all want to live a happy and peaceful life. I would be glad to give you lots of money if you are willing to retire. You can buy land, build houses and have as many pretty women as you want. You and I will remain friends, and there will never be any mistrust between us. Wouldn't it be?"

The following day all the generals submitted their resignation. Taizu bestowed noble titles and fine estates upon each one of them.

110

COMMENT: Power was traded for wealth and peace of mind. For Taizu, there would be no contenders for the throne. For the generals, there would be no suspicious ruler behind their back. It was a deal that brought benefit to both sides.

宋太祖说："人生苦短。每个人都希望快快乐乐，太太平平过一辈子。如果你们愿意退休的话，我会赏给你们许多金银。你们可以购置田产，娶美女，想要几个，就娶几个。你们退休了，你我还是朋友。我们君臣之间没有猜疑，上下相安，不是很好吗？"

第二天，所有的将领都请求辞职。宋太祖给每个人都封了官衔，并赏赐给他们大量的财物。

点评：将领们用权力换取了财富和心境的平安。宋太祖不用担心有人和他争夺皇位，将领们也不用担心宋太祖在背后对他们有猜疑。这是一笔对双方都合算的交易。

天
tiān
sky; heaven; day

在一个手脚伸开的人上面加了一横线表示头，引申为天。
A horizontal stroke is added to a man stretching his limbs to indicate the head. It came to mean the sky by extension.

8

FIRING AND HIRING

Li Ji was a distinguished general under Emperor Taizong, the founder of the Tang dynasty, and was utterly loyal to him. But Taizong, who was in declining health, was not sure Li Ji would be as loyal to his son after his death. He asked Defense Minister Li Jing for advice.

"You told me Li Ji is a very capable commander. But can he be trusted? I wonder if he should still be on the job when I am no longer around. Frankly, I don't know whether the crown prince can control him."

His question put Li Jing in a delicate position. If he told the emperor not to doubt Li Ji's loyalty, the emperor might think he was partial to his subordinate. Neither could he say that Li Ji was not to be trusted.

Li Jing came up with an idea. "Your Majesty will please dismiss Li Ji and let the crown prince hire him back later. This way he will always be grateful to the prince. I can't see any harm in doing so."

"Excellent!" exclaimed Taizong.

Shortly afterwards he demoted General Li Ji to the position of a provincial prefect. Li Ji seemed able to read Taizong's mind. He went straight to his new post from work without even going home.

Four months later, Taizong died. His heir, Zhi, called Li Ji

8

忠　诚

李勣是唐太宗手下一名杰出的将领，对太宗忠心耿耿。太宗身体日渐虚弱。他没有把握自己死后李勣对他的儿子会不会照样忠心不贰。为此，他征询兵部尚书李靖的意见。

"你说李勣能用兵，但他靠得住吗？我不知道我死了以后该不该让他留任。说实话，我不知道太子是否管得住他。"

太宗的问题使李靖左右为难。如果他说太宗不应该怀疑李勣，太宗会认为他偏袒部下。但是，他又不能说李勣不可信任。

于是，他想出了一个主意。"陛下不妨将李勣免职，日后再让太子重新起用他。这样一来，李勣一定会感恩图报。我看不出这样做有什么不好。"

太宗高兴地说："很好。"

没多久，太宗把李勣降职到外省去做官。李勣似乎猜到太宗的心思。他接到任命后，连家都没回，就直接去赴任。

四个月后，太宗病故，太子李治即位。他将李勣召回，

back and appointed him chief minister.

COMMENT: Loyalty is an honorable trait and must be earned in honorable ways. There is nothing to recommend trying to earn a man's loyalty with duplicitous means.

任命他为司空。

点评：忠诚是一种高尚的品质。必须光明磊落地赢得他人的忠诚才对。像唐太宗那样用欺骗手段赚取别人的忠诚，是不可取的。

115

仁 rén humanity; benevolence	仁的左边是人，右边是二。说明人与人之间要相亲相爱。 The left side of the ideograph refers to man and the right side is the word "two." Together they refer to what should govern the relationship between men, i.e., love and humanity.

9

BALANCE OF POWER

Duke Huan, the ruler of Qi, intended to bestow the title of Lord Uncle on Guan Zhong who was his prime minister. He sought opinion from his advisors.

"Those who are opposed to my idea, please stand on the right," he said, "and those who are in favor, please stand on the left."

Dongguo Ya stood in the middle of the doorway.

"What do you mean?" asked the duke.

"In Your Highness's opinion, is Guan Zhong capable of running the country?"

"Yes, he is."

"Is he decisive enough to carry out a great plan?"

"Sure, he is."

"Do you feel safe when he combines his ability with the sweeping power that comes with the new title?"

Duke Huan took the point. He split Guan Zhong's power among the ministers and nobody had an overriding authority.

COMMENT: While checks and balances are necessary in an organization to prevent the abuse of power, an organization fraught with checks and balances may be self-defeating when swift action is called for such as in a time of crisis. Too many checks and balances can be as bad as too few.

9

管仲的权力

齐桓公打算尊管仲为仲父。

他吩咐群臣说:"赞成我主张的,进门请靠左边站;不赞成的,请靠右边站。"

东郭牙站在门的当中。

桓公问:"你为什么站在门当中?"

东郭牙说:"主公以为管仲的智慧能治理天下吗?"

桓公说:"能。"

"主公以为管仲的决断敢发动大事吗?"

桓公说:"敢。"

东郭牙说:"以管仲的才华加上他的新头衔带来的权势,主公感到安全吗?"

桓公觉得东郭牙的话很有道理,就把管仲的权力分给几位大臣,使他们互相牵制。

点评:任何组织对权力都应该有一定的制衡,以防权力的滥用。但是,如果一个组织有太多的制衡,在发生危机,需要果敢行动时,就可能失败。太多或太少的制衡都不可取。

10

DELEGATING

Fu Zijian was appointed governor of Danfu in Shandong. He was concerned that Duke Ai, the ruler of Lu, might listen to his opponents in court and hinder him in his work. He came up with an idea and asked the duke to send two of his aides to come with him to Danfu.

The local officials all came out to greet him. Fu Zijian told the two aides to make a record. When they were writing, he pulled at their elbows. As a result, they could not write properly. Fu Zijian scolded them for poor handwriting and sent them back.

The two men reported what happened to Duke Ai.

"I got his message," the duke said. "He was telling me not to interfere with his work."

The duke sent a letter to Fu Zijian, telling him that he had a free hand running Danfu and might report back in five years.

As governor of Danfu, Fu Zijian did not seem very busy. In fact, he had time to play the lute everyday. Nevertheless, Danfu was well run.

He was succeeded by Wu Maqi. Governor Wu worked from morning till night, but there seemed to be no end of problems. Frustrated, he called on Fu Zijian for advice.

"I heard when you were the governor, you had time to play music and everything was fine. I spend all my time on my job

10

宓子贱治亶父

宓子贱被任命为山东亶父的县官。他担心鲁哀公听信他朝中对手的谗言而妨碍他的工作，就请鲁哀公派两名近侍和他一起到亶父去。

亶父的地方官员都来参见宓子贱。宓子贱叫这两个人做记录，却在他们写字的时候，不时地拉扯他们的膀子，结果他们写不好字。宓子贱就发脾气，把他们送了回去。

两个人回去后，向鲁哀公报告了事情的经过。

鲁哀公说："我知道了。宓子贱是拿这件事来叫我不要干涉他。"

鲁哀公写信给宓子贱，告诉他可以放手地治理亶父，五年以后再做汇报。

宓子贱担任亶父县官时，看上去并不忙，他还有时间弹琴。但亶父却治理得很好。

他的后任巫马期从早忙到晚，问题却层出不穷。

于是他请教宓子贱。"我听说你当县官的时候，一切都治理得很好，你还有时间奏乐。我把所有的时间都用在工作上，可是工作仍然不顺手。你有什么秘诀？"

but things are still not going well. What's the secret of your success?"

"I trust my subordinates and delegate responsibilities to them," Fu Zijian replied. "But you prefer to take on everything yourself. No wonder you are exhausted, and you still can't do a good job. Learn to delegate. It will make a world of difference."

COMMENT: If a man has no self-confidence and no sense of security, he won't be able to trust others and delegate.

宓子贱回答说:"我信任下属,把任务交给他们,而你事必躬亲。难怪你做得很累,却还是做不好。你要学会放权给别人。结果会大不相同。"

点评:如果一个人没有自信心和安全感,他是不可能信任别人,也不可能放权给别人的。

121

木
mù
tree; wood

此字有树枝,树干和树根,的确像一棵树。
The pictograph of a tree with the branches, the roots and the trunk.

11

HEIRS TO GREATNESS

Xiao He was prime minister under Liu Bang, founder of the Han dynasty. He implemented a series of highly effective policies that laid the foundation of the Han which was to become a great dynasty lasting more than four hundred years.

After his death, his successor Cao Shen faithfully followed in his footsteps, but did not do much else. Emperor Hui, who succeeded Liu Bang, was not impressed. He upbraided Cao Shen for not working hard enough.

"Who is smarter, Your Majesty or Gaozu?" Cao Shen asked. Gaozu was the posthumous title for Liu Bang, meaning the great ancestor.

"How can I be compared with Gaozu?"

"Who is more capable, I or Xiao He?"

"I don't think you are as good as Xiao He."

"Exactly. Since Gaozu and Xiao He have laid down very successful policies, the best we can do is to adhere to them and make sure we don't make mistakes, isn't it?"

Emperor Hui agreed.

COMMENT: While heirs to greatness may not be able to build greatness on top of greatness, they can do well if they follow the success recipe of their predecessors.

11

萧规曹随

　　萧何是汉朝开国皇帝刘邦的相国。他实行了一系列有效的政策，为汉朝的江山打下了基础，创立了汉朝历时四百多年的伟业。

　　萧何死后，曹参做了相国。他按照萧何的做法治理国家，别的什么都不管。刘邦的后任汉惠帝不以为然。他责怪曹参治国不够努力。

　　曹参说："请问皇上，您跟高祖比，哪一位更英明？"高祖是刘邦的谥号。

　　汉惠帝说："我哪里比得上高祖呢？"

　　曹参又问："我跟萧何比，哪一位更贤明？"

　　汉惠帝说："你不如萧何。"

　　曹参说："皇上说得完全对。既然高祖和萧何制定了很成功的政策，我们只要照着办，不出差错，不就很好吗？"

　　汉惠帝认为曹参言之有理。

点评：伟人的接班人未必能超越前任的伟大。但如果他们能遵循前任成功的做法，也可以做得不错。

12

AFFIRMATIVE WORDS

Liu Pin was appointed the magistrate of a backward region in Sichuan in the Tang dynasty. The local residents were mostly poor and uneducated. One day the son of a junior officer came to visit and showed him some essays he had written. Liu Pin complimented the man on his work and often honorably mentioned him in public.

His aides were bewildered. They did not understand why Liu Pin praised him so much, for the man's essays were mediocre at best.

"Here is a young man who came from an illiterate family," Liu Pin explained, "but is devoted to learning. He studied very hard on his own. I must not discourage him. Because of my praise, his peers will be impressed and follow his example. He himself will surely work even harder. If a lot of people do the same, life in this region will improve. And there will be fewer law-breakers. Why should I be stingy with my praise?"

COMMENT: Don't you agree that Liu Pin was rather progressive in his thinking? His praise would give the young man confidence about himself, and such confidence might well spur him on to genuine success.

12

柳玭的表扬

　　唐朝时，柳玭担任四川省一个落后地区的郡守。当地的居民大多贫穷，没有文化。有一次，一个都校的儿子拿着自己写的文章来见他。柳玭称赞了他，还经常表扬他。柳玭的下属想不通。此人的文章很一般，为什么柳玭要表扬他呢？

　　柳玭说："这个年轻人家里都不识字。他偏偏爱读书，而且非常用功。我必须鼓励他。因为我称赞他，别人就会看重他，模仿他。他自己也会越发上进。如果很多人都和他一样，我们这个地方的民生就会改善，犯罪的人就会减少。我何必舍不得说几句表扬的话呢？"

点评：你不觉得柳玭的思想相当进步吗？他的表扬会带给这个年轻人自信，而这种自信又会促使他获得真实的成就。

13

AFFIRMATIVE ACTION

In the Ming dynasty, civil servants were selected on the basis of the imperial examinations just like the Tang and Song dynasties before.

Traditionally southern China was culturally more advanced than northern China. As a result, those who passed the imperial examinations had mostly been southerners. The result of the examination in 1397 was more extreme. Not a single northerner passed the exam. This caused an outcry among northerners who accused the chief examiner, a southerner, of discriminating against them.

The founding emperor, Zhu Yuanzhang, ordered an investigation which revealed no foul play. Nevertheless the northerners were not satisfied and social unrest was looming. The emperor decided to allow sixty-two northerners to pass the examination because northerners were needed in the civil service to help maintain social order and political stability in the north.

It was not until twenty-five years later that imbalance was redressed once and for all. Under the instruction of Emperor Renzong, the fourth emperor of Ming, his ministers devised a quota system to guarantee that there would be forty northerners and sixty southerners every year to pass the imperial examinations.

Emperor Renzong was satisfied with the new system. He

13

南北榜之争

明朝在选官制度上沿用了唐宋以来的科举制度。

唐宋以来，中国南方文化较发达。因此，南方人在科举考试中总是占优势。考中进士的大多数是南方人，北方人考中的很少。

洪武三十年春的科举更为极端。那一年，北方人全部落选。北方人十分不满，纷纷指责南方籍的主考官包庇南人，压抑北人。事情闹得很凶。

明朝开国皇帝朱元璋为查明真相，派员调查。经认真核查，并没有发现舞弊行为。然而，北方人仍是不服。朱元璋考虑到需要北方人稳定北方社会和政局，所以钦定了六十二名北方人为进士。

南北榜之争，直到二十五年之后，才一劳永逸地得到解决。大臣们根据明朝第四个皇帝仁宗的指示，制定了相关办法以确保南北兼收。每年科举规定取南人六十名，北人四十名。

仁宗很高兴。他说："往年科举，北人因很少考中，不免沮丧。在新的制度下，北人也将努力学习，奋发图强了。"

said, "Northerners will be discouraged if they cannot pass the examination. Under the new system, they will be motivated to work hard and make a career in the civil service."

The quota system was later refined. The examination paper of each candidate would be marked "South", "North", and "Central" according to where he came from and successful candidates were selected from each province to work in the civil service. Consequently the rule of the central government was strengthened.

The Qing dynasty, which succeeded the Ming, kept the system.

COMMENT: The affirmative action taken by the emperor addressed the very purpose of the imperial examination which was to select civil servants. While it might be unfair to southerners, the affirmative action served a larger purpose of the nation.

后来，南北分省取士的制度作了进一步的改革。会试分为"南"、"北"、"中"三卷。科举考试的这一改革，改变了录取名额的不平衡状况，保证各省人士都有机会进入行政机构，从而加强了中央政府的统治。

清朝也承袭明制，实行南北分省取士的办法。

点评：南北分省取士达到了科举选官的目的。也许这一制度对南方人有失公允，但是对整个国家却有好处。

129

林 lín woods;　森 sēn forest

两棵树表示树林。三棵树表示茂密的树林。
Two trees together conveys the idea of a wood. Three trees together means a dense wood or forest.

PART IV

MANAGING HUMAN RESOURCES

管理人才资源

1

RECOMMENDATION

Duke Ping, the ruler of Jin, asked his minister, Qi Huangyang, to recommend a candidate for the governorship of Nanyang.

"Xie Hu is the most suitable candidate," Qi Huangyang suggested without hesitation.

"But isn't he your opponent?" The duke wondered.

"Your Highness asked me who would be the best candidate to run Nanyang. You did not ask me who my adversary was."

"True. I'll appoint Xie Hu."

Just as Qi Huangyang had expected, Xie Hu did a good job running Nanyang.

Some time later the duke asked Qi Huangyang to recommend a judge for the court.

"Qi Wu will do the job well," said he without hesitation.

"But he is your son. How can you recommend your own son? What will other people say?"

"Your Highness asked me who would be the most qualified man to sit on the bench. You didn't ask me whether he was my son."

"True."

Qi Wu was duly appointed. He proved to be a fair and hard-working judge and earned public approval.

1

祁黄羊荐亲

晋平公问大夫祁黄羊："谁担任南阳县的县官比较合适？"

祁黄羊不假思索地回答："解狐很合适。"

晋平公感到很奇怪："解狐不是你的对手吗？"

"大王问的是谁适合做南阳县的县官，没有问谁是我的对手啊。"

"你说得有道理。我就让解狐去当县官吧。"

正如祁黄羊所预期的，解狐干得很出色。

过了不久，晋平公要祁黄羊推荐一名法官。

祁黄羊毫不犹豫地回答："祁午可以胜任。"

"祁午不是你的儿子吗？你怎么能够推荐自己的儿子呢？别人会怎么说啊？"

"大王问的是谁能胜任法官这个职位，没有问谁是我的儿子啊。"

"好吧。"

于是，祁午当上了法官。他断案公正，办事勤勉，获得了朝廷上下的一致好评。

COMMENT: Confucius praised Qi Huangyang for being a man without bias, who recommended people without prejudice and without fear of being accused of nepotism and did not let personal feelings interfere with his consideration.

点评：孔子称赞祁黄羊，说他公正而没有偏见，外举不避仇，内举不避亲，推荐人才毫无私心。

135

本
běn
root;
foundation

"木"字底部加一画表示树根。
A short line is added to the base of a tree to indicate where the roots are.

2

WIFELY WISDOM

King Zhuang of Chu was so fond of hunting he often neglected his work. His wife, Lady Fan, admonished him, but he turned a deaf ear to her. So she refused to eat any game he brought back. The king eventually gave up hunting.

One day the king came home late. Lady Fan asked why.

"I had a very interesting conversation in the palace."

"Who were you talking with?"

"Prime Minister Yu Qiuzi."

Lady Fan sneered.

"Why did you sneer?"

"I don't think Yu Qiuzi is a loyal minister."

"What do you mean?"

"Well, I've been your wife for eleven years. I often recruit pretty women for you. I am never jealous of them or afraid they may compete with me for your favor. Now Yu Qiuzi has been your prime minister for ten years. But I've never heard him recommending anybody. If he knows a talented man but does not recommend him to you, he is not loyal to you. If he does not know any one to recommend, he is not doing his job. Such a man I can only laugh at."

When the king told him of Lady Fan's remarks, Yu Qiuzi was at a loss what to say. Shortly after that he handed in his

2

樊　姬

　　楚庄王喜欢打猎，常常忽略政事。他的夫人樊姬进谏劝止，庄王不听，樊姬就不吃猎物的肉。庄王于是不再打猎。

　　有一天，庄王散朝晚了。樊姬问他是什么原因。

　　"我在宫里谈得很有兴致。"

　　"您跟谁谈话？"

　　"宰相虞丘子。"

　　樊姬鄙夷地笑了笑。

　　"你笑什么？"

　　"虞丘子不是一位忠臣。"

　　"你是什么意思？"

　　樊姬回答说："我侍奉大王有十一年了。我经常搜求美女进献给大王。我既不嫉妒她们，也不害怕她们争宠。虞丘子做了十年宰相。可是我从来没有听说过他推荐什么人。如果他知道有贤人而不推荐，他是不忠；如果他不知道有贤人，他是不称职。我笑这样的人，有什么不可以呢？"

　　庄王把樊姬的话告诉给了虞丘子。虞丘子无言以对。

resignation and recommended Sun Shu-ao to take his place. Under Sun Shu-ao, Qi was well-run and enjoyed unprecedented prosperity.

COMMENT: Would you recommend somebody more capable than you to your boss? The answer has much to do with your sense of self-worth and self-confidence.

没多久，他提出辞呈，推荐孙叔敖为宰相。在孙叔敖的治理下，楚国变得国富民强。

点评：你会把一个比你更能干的人推荐给上司吗？你的回答将显示你的自信和心胸。

末
mò
end; tip

"木"字上端加一画表示树梢。
A short line is added to the upper part of a tree to indicate the tip of the tree.

3

DEAD HORSE

Since Yan was defeated by Qi, King Zhao was bent on taking revenge on his foe. He wanted to recruit men of talent to work for him and make Yan a strong country. He asked Mr. Guo Wei for advice.

Guo Wei said, "If your ambition is to rule an empire, you work with your mentors. If your ambition is to rule a kingdom, you work with your friends. If your ambition is to be a warlord, you work with your subjects. And the loser mixes himself with those who are only fit to be his servants."

"What should I do to attract talents?"

"If you wait upon them with humility, you'll attract those who are a hundred times better than you. If you are the first to come to work and the last to take a rest, you'll attract those who are ten times better than you. If others run and you run as fast as them, you'll attract those who are as good as you are. If you order them about with a stick, you'll only attract those who are fit to be your servants. To enlist the able and virtuous, you must call upon them yourself."

"Who should I call upon first?"

"Let me tell you a story. An ancient king loved horses. He offered a thousand ounces of gold for a stallion that could run a thousand *li* a day. But for three years he was unable to get one. A courtier offered to travel around the country to look for one.

3

千里马招贤

　　自从燕国被齐国打败以后，燕昭王一心要报仇雪恨。他希望招贤纳士，把燕国建成一个强国。为此，他向郭隗先生请教。

　　郭隗说："如果你想建立帝业，你就和老师一起努力。如果你想建立王业，你就和朋友一起努力。如果你想建立霸业，你就和臣子一起努力。亡国之君则和奴仆之类的人厮混在一起。"

　　燕昭王问："我如何能网罗到人才呢？"

　　郭隗说："如果你谦卑地事奉贤人，比你强一百倍的人就会来。如果你工作在人先，休息在人后，比你强十倍的人就会来。如果别人跑，你和别人跑得一样快，跟你一样水平的人就会来。如果你拿着一根棍子，颐指气使，发号施令，奴仆之类的人就会来。你要招募贤人，必须亲自拜访他们。"

　　燕昭王问："我应当先拜访谁呢？"

　　郭隗回答说："我给你讲个故事吧。古时候有一个国王喜欢马。他愿意以千金的高价征求一匹千里马。可是买了三年也没有买到。一个侍臣要求国王让他到各地

The king gave him a grand sum of money for the purchase. Three months later the courtier came back with the bones of a dead horse that reputedly ran a thousand *li* a day when it was alive. He paid five hundred ounces of gold for its remains.

"The king was furious. 'I want a live horse. Why did you waste my money on a dead one?'

"'Your Majesty, if people know you are willing to pay five hundred ounces for a dead horse, I'm sure you'll find a fast horse soon.'

"In less than a year the king was able to obtain three very fast horses."

Guo Wei went on to say, "Now if Your Majesty wants to attract talented men, you should start with me. I'm not that talented. If I am given a senior position and treated well, those who are more capable than I will definitely come to you."

The king built a mansion for Guo Wei and treated him respectfully as though Guo Wei were his tutor. As the word spread, many talented men came to offer him their service. Among them the most famous was Yue Yi who eventually helped the king conquer Qi, wiping out the humiliation of defeat.

COMMENT: Gou Wei's advice on people management contains immortal truth, and the fable of the dead horse is perennially instructive.

去寻找千里马，国王给了他一大笔钱。过了三个月，这个人用五百两金子买回了一具千里马的尸骨。国王大怒。

"'我要的是活马，你为什么花钱买死马呢？'

"'主公，如果人们知道你连一匹死马都愿意花五百两金子，那么你很快就会买到一匹活的千里马。'

"果然不到一年，国王买到了三匹千里马。"

郭隗接着说："如果主公有诚意招贤纳士，那么就从我开始吧。我没有什么才能，如果我都被主公重用，那么，比我能力强的人一定会来投奔主公。"

燕昭王就为郭隗建了一座豪宅，像对待老师一样对待他。果然，天下的贤人争先恐后地来投奔燕昭王，其中最著名的是乐毅。他最终帮助燕昭王打败了齐国，雪了辱国之耻。

143

点评：臣役之对，天下之格言。市马之喻，万世之美谈。

4

SHEEPSKIN

Duke Mu, the ruler of Qin, married a princess of Jin. Included in her dowry was a slave named Bai Lixi, who had been a minister of Yu. When Yu was wiped out by Jin, Bai Lixi became a slave.

On his way to Qin, Bai Lixi managed to escape. But when he passed through Chu, he was taken for a spy and got arrested.

Duke Mu asked the man who escorted the dowry who Bai Lixi was.

"He is a man of outstanding talent, but has no luck."

Duke Mu ordered an inquiry and found out that Bai Lixi was made a slave to attend cows in Chu. Thereupon he prepared some expensive gifts to offer to the king of Chu in exchange for the man. His minister Gongsun Zhi stopped him.

"If the king of Chu knows you are willing to pay this much for a slave, he will realize Bai Lixi is no common man. He may want to keep him to himself."

The duke took his advice and sent an envoy to Chu with five pieces of sheepskin, which was the market price for a slave.

"Bai Lixi is wanted in Qin for a crime," the envoy told the king. "Please hand him over. We want to punish him."

The king of Chu took the sheepskin and handed over Bai Lixi.

Duke Mu was disappointed when he saw a hoary-haired

4

五张羊皮

秦穆公娶了晋国的公主。在公主的陪嫁品里，有一个名叫百里奚的人。百里奚原是虞国的大臣，虞国被晋国灭亡以后，当了奴隶。

在去秦国的途中，百里奚偷偷地逃跑了。可是他经过楚国时，被当作奸细抓了起来。

秦穆公问运送嫁妆的官员百里奚是什么人。

那官员回答说："他是一个非常有才华的人，可惜怀才不遇。"

秦穆公派人四处寻访，打听到百里奚在楚国养牛，就准备了贵重的礼品，打算送给楚王，把百里奚换回来，但被大臣公孙枝阻止了。

公孙枝说："如果楚王知道你愿意为一个奴隶付如此重金，他必然明白百里奚不是常人，就不会放他出来。"

秦穆公恍然大悟，就派使者按照当时一个奴隶的市价，带了五张羊皮去见楚王。

使者对楚王说："百里奚在秦国犯了法，请让我们把他赎回去受惩。"

楚王收下羊皮，把百里奚交给了秦国的使者。

old man brought in.

"How old are you?" he asked Bai Lixi.

"I am seventy years old."

"Ah, I'm afraid you are too old, sir."

"If you want me to fight a tiger, my lord, then I am too old. But if you want me to help you run the government, I don't think I am too old."

Duke Mu felt he had a point. He had a long conversation with Bai Lixi. At the end of it, he was convinced that Bai was a rare talent and appointed him co-prime minister.

COMMENT: The value of a piece of merchandise lies in its perception and the perception can be manipulated.

秦穆王看见百里奚满头白发，有些失望。

"先生多大年纪了？"

"我今年七十岁。"

"唉，可惜先生太老了。"

百里奚说："如果主公派我上山打老虎，我确实是太老了。但是，如果用我帮助主公治理国家，那我并不老。"

秦穆公感到他的话有道理，就邀请他长谈。结果，他深信百里奚是一位难得的人才，就任命他当宰相。

147

点评：一件商品的价值取决于人们对它的看法，而人们的看法又是可以被操纵的。

果
guǒ
fruit

此字描绘一棵果实累累的树。
The pictograph of a fruit-bearing tree.

5

REDEEMING A SLAVE

Yan Ying, prime minister of Qi, saw a man taking a rest by the road with a bundle of firewood beside him. But he did not look like a common laborer.

"What's your name?" asked Yan Ying. "What do you do for a living?"

"My name is Yue Shifu. I am an indentured slave."

Yan Ying took pity on him. He redeemed him from his master for the cost of a horse and invited him to ride with him. When he got home, Yan Ying went straight in without a word, leaving Yue Shifu at the gate. He did not come out for a long while. Yue Shifu was offended and declared that he would have nothing to do with Yan Ying.

Yan Ying was upset. "I've just met you. But I redeemed you. Isn't that good enough? Why are you so easily offended?"

"A gentleman can put up with those who don't understand him," Yue Shifu replied, "but will expect to be treated as equal by those who do. I've been working as a slave for three years. Nobody knew me or cared for me. Since you redeemed me, I thought you were my friend. But you didn't treat me like a gentleman. You were not courteous when we were riding in the carriage. I thought you just overlooked your manners. You were outright rude to keep me waiting for so long outside your house. I'd rather be somebody else's slave than be treated like a

5

晏婴赎奴

齐相晏婴看见路边有一个人在休息，身旁放着一捆柴，但这人看上去不像一般的民工。

晏婴问他："你叫什么名字？是做什么的？"

"我叫越石夫，是别人家的奴隶。"

晏婴怜悯他，就用一匹马的价钱把他从主人那里赎了出来。然后，邀他一起坐车同行。到了家，晏婴不打招呼，就径自走了进去，将越石夫留在大门口等候。过了很长时间，晏婴才出来。越石夫生气了，他告诉晏婴今后不想再跟他来往。

晏婴感到很委屈，便说："我刚见到你，就把你赎了出来，你怎么一下子就生气了？"

越石夫说："君子可以容忍不理解他的人，但期待那些理解他的人对他平等相待。我做了三年奴隶，没有人知道我，关心我。承您把我赎出来，我以为您是知己。可是您并没有把我当君子对待。刚才我们一起坐马车的时候，您就不礼貌。我想您可能一时疏忽。现在，您让我在屋外等了这么久。您分明是不尊重人。我宁可当别人的奴隶，也不愿被一个我视为朋友的人

slave by someone whom I take for a friend."

Yan Ying immediately apologized and treated Yue Shifu like a guest of honor. Yue Shifu proved a man of great ability and integrity.

COMMENT: To treat those who receive your help with dignity is not only good manner, but good character.

像奴隶一样对待。"

晏婴听了这番话以后，马上请越石夫原谅，把他奉为上宾。后来的事实表明，越石夫的确是一位贤能的人。

点评：尊敬那些接受你帮助的人，不仅说明你有礼貌，而且说明你有好品德。

休
xiū
rest

此字左边是人，右边是树，指一个人靠在树身上休息。
The left side of the character is a man and the right side a tree. It means a man leaning against a tree to rest.

6

A FRIGHTENED BIRD

The king of Zhao sent his envoy, Wei Jia, to Chu to discuss their alliance against Qin. In a meeting with Lord Chunshen, prime minister of Chu, Wei Jia asked him who would lead Chu's army.

"Lord Linwu will be the commander."

Wei Jia frowned at Lord Linwu's name. "I was fond of archery when I was young. If you don't mind, I'd like to tell you a story about archery."

"Please do."

"One day General Geng Lei was accompanying the king of Wei on a hunting excursion. Seeing a wild goose come flying from the east, he said to the king, 'I can shoot down the bird with an empty bow.'

"'An empty bow? With no arrow?'

"'Yes, Your Majesty.'

"At that moment the goose came near. Geng Lei raised his bow, aimed at it and pulled the string. Twang! The bird fell as though it had been hit by an arrow.

"The king was surprised. 'How did you do that?'

"'The bird was already wounded by an arrow.'

"'How do you know?'

"'I noticed it was flying with difficulty, falling behind its companions. Its painful calls told me it had been wounded.

6

惊弓之鸟

赵王派魏加去楚国商议抗秦联盟的事宜，魏加拜见楚相春申君时，问他谁将统领楚军。

春申君说："临武君将担任楚军统帅。"

魏加皱了皱眉头说："臣年轻时喜欢射箭，臣想给阁下说个射箭的故事。"

"请讲。"

"有一天，魏将更羸陪魏王打猎，看见空中有一只野雁飞过来。

"他对魏王说：'我不用箭就能把它射下来。'

"'你只用一张空弓？没有箭？'

"'是的，大王。'

"这时，那只大雁已经飞近。更羸拉开弓，向飞来的雁虚拨了一下弓弦。那只雁果然随着弦响掉落在地。

"魏王惊奇地问：'先生箭术果然高明。你是怎么打下它的？'

"更羸说：'其实这只鸟已经受过箭伤。'

"'你怎么知道？'

"'我注意到它飞得很吃力，落在同伴后面。叫的声

When I pulled the bowstring, the twang frightened it because it thought another arrow was coming. As it was making a desperate attempt to dodge the arrow, the old wound burst. So it fell from the sky.'

"Now to come back to what we were talking. Lord Linwu has been beaten by Qin's army. He may have a lingering fear. If I were you, I wouldn't reappoint him."

COMMENT: This might not be the case. If Lord Linwu had learned from his experience, he could well do a better job next time.

154

音又凄惨，说明它受了伤。我一拉弓，它听见弓弦的声音，以为又有一支箭要射过来，就吓得拼命躲开，结果旧伤破裂，从空中掉了下来。'

"现在，回到我们刚才的话题。临武君曾被秦军打败，心里一定害怕秦军。换了我，就不会派他担任楚军的将领去抗击秦军。"

点评：这未必如此。如果临武君能够吸取失败的教训，他下一次完全有可能打胜仗。

山
shān
mountain; hill

此字表示一座有三个高峰的山。
The pictograph of a mountain with three peaks.

7

ARMCHAIR GENERAL

Zhao Kuo's father was a brilliant general of Zhao. Zhao Kuo studied the art of war since he was a boy and became so eloquent that he even beat his father in their discussion on the subject. But his father did not think he could make a good general. Zhao Kuo's mother asked to know the reason.

"War is a matter of life and death," said the father. "But our son makes light of it. I hope he'll never be an army general."

After his father's death, Zhao Kuo became an officer. When Qin invaded Zhao, the king wanted to appoint him as the commander-in-chief to fight the enemy. His mother implored the king not to do so.

"His father took good care of his men. Whatever Your Majesty gave him, he shared with the rank and file soldiers. He was totally devoted to his job and never allowed other things to divert his mind. But Zhao Kuo is different. He has only book knowledge of the art of war and doesn't know how to apply it in real battle. Yet he is arrogant. He doesn't share what Your Majesty gives him with his soldiers, but is keen on buying properties for himself. You will make a grave mistake appointing him."

"Leave it to me, madam," the king said. "I've made up my mind."

7

纸上谈兵

赵括的父亲是赵国的名将。赵括自幼学习兵法，他谈论兵法战略，连父亲也难不倒他。但是父亲并不认为儿子是将才。赵括的母亲问这是什么道理。父亲说："战争是关乎生死的大事，但是括儿说得轻松容易，我希望他永远不要带领军队。"

父亲死了以后，赵括当了一名军官。当秦国侵犯赵国时，国王任命赵括为赵军的统帅。赵括的母亲力图劝阻赵王。

"他的父亲很照顾将士。陛下赏赐的财物，全都分给将士们享用。每次出征，他一心一意地筹划军机，从不过问家务。但是赵括不同。他只有书本知识，并不懂得如何在实战中运用兵法。他才当上将领，就架子十足。陛下赏赐的财物，他都带回家，不分给士兵，却很留意为自己购买田产。陛下千万别让他带兵。"

"夫人别说了，我已经拿定主意了。"

赵括的母亲说："如果大王一定要用他，那么将来就不要怪我没有提醒您。"

赵括担任赵军统帅以后，撤换了许多将官，又改变

"If so, I'll have nothing to do with your decision," said the mother. "Don't tell me I haven't warned you."

After taking the command of the Zhao army, Zhao Kuo replaced many earlier appointments and changed the strategy of his predecessor. The army of Qin was led by an experienced general. During the campaign, he fooled Zhao Kuo by feigning retreat, split Zhao's troops into two parts, cut their supply line and besieged them for forty days. When Zhao Kuo tried to break through the siege, he was killed and his army sustained a devastating defeat. The army of Qin almost overran the capital of Zhao.

COMMENT: As few people know a man better than his parents, their warning should never be dismissed.

了军队的策略。秦国的统帅是一员沙场老将。他在交战中假装战败退走，用计将赵国的军队一截为二，切断赵军的补给线，将赵军围困了四十天。赵括率部突围时，被秦军杀死，全军溃败。赵国的首都也差一点被秦军占领。

点评：知子莫如父母亲。评估人才时，应当重视父母亲对他们的看法。

川
chuān
river

此字看上去就像河里的流水。
The pictograph of a river. It looks like water flowing in a river.

8

TWO WEAKNESSES

Guan Zhong was recommended to the ruler of Qi, Duke Huan, by the duke's mentor. The interview lasted three days. So impressed was the duke that he appointed Guan Zhong prime minister.

"I must admit I have two weaknesses," the duke told Guan Zhong. "I'm fond of hunting and I'm fond of women. Do you think they would prevent me from being a great ruler?"

"No, they won't."

"What will hinder my success?"

"If you don't know how to identify men of talent and virtue."

"Well, I believe I have identified a few. What will hinder my success then?"

"If you don't trust and make good use of them."

"I don't think that's the case."

"Thing can still go wrong if you place them in important positions but make mean men work side by side and interfere with them."

Duke Huan assured Guan Zhong of his confidence in him and delegated much of the decision-making to him.

Under Guan Zhong's management, Qi became one of the most powerful states in China. Duke Huan ruled the country for forty-three years and became one of the most influential

8

齐桓公的弱点

齐桓公的老师向他推荐管仲。齐桓公跟管仲谈了三天，对管仲极其器重，拜他为相国。

齐桓公问管仲："我有两个大弱点。我爱打猎又好色。你认为这两点会妨碍我做一个伟大的君主吗？

"不会。"

"那么什么会阻碍我呢？"

"不知贤。"

"我已经找到了几位贤人。什么还会妨碍我呢？"

"知贤却不信任贤，不用贤。"

"我不会。"

"还有，如果你用贤的同时又用小人去干涉他们，也会妨碍你的成功。"

水
shuǐ
water

此字原像一条河流，两旁有漩涡。
The original pictograph showed a stream with whirls of water on both sides.

politicians in the Spring and Autumn Period.

COMMENT: Big strengths outweigh small weaknesses and big weaknesses outweigh small strengths.

　　齐桓公对管仲说，他完全信任他。许多重大国策齐桓公都让管仲决定。

　　在管仲的治理下，齐国变成一个强国。齐桓公在位四十三年，是春秋时期最有影响力的政治家。

点评：大优点可以掩盖小缺点，但大缺点不是小优点所能掩盖的。

163

火
huǒ
fire

此字像一团上升的火舌。
The pictograph resembles the shape of a fire rising into the air.

9

GUAN AND BAO

When his prime minister Guan Zhong was seriously ill, Duke Huan asked him who could be his successor.

"Who do you have in mind?" Guan Zhong asked.

"Bao Shuya."

"No," Guan Zhong objected even though Bao was a great friend of his. "Bao Shuya is an upright and honest man, but he keeps away from those who are not as capable as he is. If he hears about someone's fault, he will not forget. If you appoint him prime minister, you'll find him rather intolerant. He won't get along with other people. It won't be long before you find him very annoying."

"Who would you recommend?"

"Xi Peng would be a better choice. He is a man of character. He is respectful of those above him and friendly to those below him. Despite his excellences, he is never condescending. He seeks to promote virtue by example. I believe Xi Peng would get along with other people well and do a good job for you."

COMMENT: To the extent that generosity and tolerance are inborn qualities, leadership is a natural gift.

9

管仲荐相

齐相管仲病得很重，齐桓公问他把国事托付给谁才合适。

管仲问："大王想要交给谁呢？"

"鲍叔牙。"

尽管鲍叔牙是管仲的好朋友，管仲却说："不可以。鲍叔牙为人算得上清白廉洁。但是他对于不如自己的人，从不去亲近。听到别人的过错，也不会忘记。让他当相国，他没有宽容心，不可能和他人相处得好。做不了多久，就会让您生气。"

"那么你推荐谁呢？"

"隰朋还可以。隰朋对上毕恭毕敬，对下和和气气，又能怜悯不如自己的人。他以身作则，用德行感化他人。我相信他跟同事们会相处得很好，能做好您给他的工作。"

点评：宽宏大量是一种与生俱来的品质。从这个意义上说，领导才能也是与生俱来的。

10

PROMOTION

Zhang Yong was Minister of Public Works under Emperor Zhenzong in the Song dynasty. He believed that a civil servant should be free from corruption even though he was poor, should be hard-working but not complain, should be loyal but not assert his loyalty, should be selfless but not flaunt his talents.

He made a point of promoting those who were capable but modest and quiet, while some of his colleagues liked to promote those who were better-known.

"You ought to help those who are capable and modest," Zhang Yong advised his colleagues. "Such people are generally prudent and have a sense of honor. If you promote them, they can be trusted to uphold their integrity and will rarely cause problems. Don't recommend those who are aggressive. Such people often have no principles. They are good at currying favor with their superiors. Once promoted, they will like to show off and become even more self-seeking. Their only concern is how to make gains for themselves. Eventually they'll get those who promoted them into trouble. So, what's the point of recommending them?"

COMMENT: To recognize capable but modest people is one of the traits of a good leader.

10

张咏荐贤

张咏在宋真宗时任工部尚书。他认为做官即使穷也要廉洁，即使辛苦也不要埋怨，要忠心耿耿而不刻意表现自己的忠诚，要一心为公而不炫耀自己的才能。

他专门荐举那些有能力、但为人谦虚恬淡的人做官，而他的同事却喜欢荐举那些名气大的人。

张咏说："你们应该举荐那些有才能而又谦虚的人。这种人廉洁谨慎，有羞耻心。受到举荐后，会更坚持志节，很少会出问题。不要举荐那些钻营的人。这种人往往委曲求全，谄媚取宠。一旦受到提拔，他们就会急于炫耀自己，就会争名逐利。他们唯一关心的是如何为自己谋利益。最后还会连累推荐他们的人。你们何必举荐这种人呢？"

点评：一个优秀领导者的特点之一是善于识别那些谦虚而有才华的人。

11

SAFETY IN NUMBERS

King Xuan of Qi loved flute music. He had a band of three hundred musicians playing for him. When Mr. Nan Guo applied to be a member of the ensemble, the king gladly hired him. But Mr. Nan Guo could not play. Still he got the same pay as the other players.

After the king's death, his son King Min preferred solo performance and asked the musicians to play one by one. Mr. Nan Guo was forced to quit.

COMMENT: Had Mr. Nan Guo used the time in the ensemble to learn from other musicians, his career would not have come to this abrupt end.

11

滥竽充数

齐宣王爱好竽乐。他有一支三百人的乐队。南郭先生表示愿意为齐王奏乐。齐王很高兴让他加入乐队。可实际上南郭先生不会吹竽，却混在里面照样拿报酬。

宣王死了，他的儿子湣王接位。湣王喜欢听独奏，就请乐师们一个一个演奏。南郭先生只好溜了。

点评：如果南郭先生利用在吹竽队的时间向其他乐师学习，就不至于落到一个逃之夭夭的下场。

12

FIVE CRITERIA

The ruler of Wei, Marquis Wen, had two ministers, Wei Cheng and Di Huang. Both were very capable. Unable to decide who should be appointed prime minister, he summoned Li Ke, a learned man, into his palace for consultation.

"Before a man achieves recognition," Li Ke told his host. "observe with whom he is associated; when he becomes rich, watch to whom he gives his money; when he has assumed a high position, look at whom he promotes; when he is in difficulty, notice what things he refuses to do; when he is poor, see what he does not accept. If you know these five aspects about a person, you know who should be appointed as prime minister."

"Thank you for your advice. I know who to appoint now."

On his way home, Li Ke came across Di Huang who invited him to his home for a chat. Earlier, Li Ke had recommended Di Huang to the marquis who appointed him to a senior position. Di Huang had become a friend of his ever since.

"I heard you were talking with the marquis about the candidate for prime minister," said Di Huang. "Who do you think would be appointed?"

"Wei Cheng."

"How come?" Di Huang was not pleased. "I recommended Wu Qi to the marquis, and Wu Qi did a good job in Xi He. I

12

李克的用人标准

魏文侯手下有两位大臣，翟黄和魏成，都很能干。魏文侯无法决定让谁做宰相，就召请学识渊博的李克来商议。

李克说："在平时，要观察一个人所亲近的人；当他富裕的时候，要观察他把钱给哪些人；当他显达的时候，要观察他提拔哪些人；当他困厄的时候，要观察什么是他不愿意做的事；当他贫穷的时候，要观察什么是他不愿意接受的东西。如果你了解这五个方面，就知道应该任命谁做宰相了。"

"谢谢你的指教。我知道应该让谁担任这个职务了。"

李克在回家的路上遇见翟黄。翟黄请他到家小坐。李克早些时候曾经向魏文侯推荐过翟黄。此后，翟黄便成了他的朋友。

翟黄说："听说国君今天请先生去讨论宰相的人选，你知道国君会任命谁吗？"

"魏成。"

翟黄听了很不高兴。

他说："我有什么比不上魏成呢？我把吴起推荐给

recommended Ximen Bao, and Ximen Bao did a good in Ye. I recommended Yue Yang, and Yue Yang won a great victory over Zhongshan. I also recommended a very good tutor for the marquis' son. I've done a lot for the marquis. I believe I'm better than Wei Cheng in every way."

"It's only my guess, my friend. I think Wei Cheng would be chosen because he is an uncommon man. He keeps only ten percent of his income to himself and gives away the rest to those working for him and other poor people. Those he recommended, the marquis treats them as his mentors. Those you recommended, the marquis made them ministers. The way Wei Cheng spends money shows his aspiration, and the quality of people Wei Cheng recommended shows his judgment. I don't think you can compare with him."

Di Huang bowed to his guest.

"You are right. I'm not as good as Wei Cheng. I am a shallow man." And he asked Li Ke to be his tutor.

Just as Li Ke had predicted, Marquis Wen appointed Wei Cheng as prime minister.

COMMENT: Li Ke's criteria have stood the test of time.

国君，吴起在西河干得很好；我把西门豹推荐给国君，西门豹在邺县干得很好；我推荐了乐羊，乐羊在中山国打了大胜仗；我又为太子推荐了一位好老师。我推荐的人个个都做得很出色。我有什么地方比不上魏成呢？"

"我猜想国君会选择魏成是因为魏成非同常人。魏成得到的俸禄，他自己只用十分之一，而把十分之九给了那些为他工作的人和穷人。魏成推荐的人，国君都视为老师。而你推荐的人，国君只任命为大臣。魏成用钱的方式显示了他的志向。魏成推荐的人显示了他的判断力。你哪里能够和魏成比呢？"

翟黄向李克作揖。

173

他说："我确实不如魏成。我是个浅陋的人。"

于是翟黄拜李克为师。

正如李克所预言的，魏文侯任命魏成为宰相。

点评：李克的用人标准历久而弥新。

PART V

MANAGING OPPONENTS

管理对手

1

DRUMBEAT

In 684 B.C., Qi declared war on Lu. A native of Lu named Cao Gui sought an audience with Duke Zhuang, the ruler of the country.

"Your Highness, what have you got to fight the enemy with?" Cao Gui asked.

"I've got loyal followers. I share food and clothing with them rather than keep it to myself."

"But they are only a handful. The people of Lu may not rally around you."

"When I pray to God, I place emphasis on sincerity rather than on the amount of offering."

"But there is no guarantee God will bless you."

"I'm not able to review every legal case, but I always strive to be fair and reasonable."

"Good. That will win the loyalty of the people. If the people are loyal to you, you can fight the enemy and win."

The armies of Qi and Lu confronted each other at Changshao, near modern Laiwu in Shandong. Duke Zhuang was about to give orders to beat the drums to launch an attack when he was stopped by Cao Gui who was riding with him in his chariot.

"Please wait."

Then the army of Qi sounded its drums. Duke Zhuang wanted to respond, but was stopped by Cao Gui again.

1

一鼓作气

公元前 684 年，齐国向鲁国宣战。鲁国人曹刿求见鲁庄公。

曹刿问："主公靠什么跟敌人打仗？"

"我有一批忠于我的人。我平时吃的穿的不敢独享，总是分给他们。"

"他们的人数很少。鲁国的百姓未必都团结在你身边。"

"我祭祀神明，靠的是诚信，而不是祭品的多少。"

"但是神明未必保佑你。"

"我虽然不能审理每一宗狱案，但我总是尽心尽力做到公平合理。"

"好，凭这一点，您能够赢得百姓的忠心。有了百姓的忠心，您就能够战胜敌人。"

齐鲁两国在长勺（即今山东莱芜）交锋。鲁庄公正要下令击鼓进攻，却被同行的曹刿制止。

"请等一等。"

这时，齐军击鼓出战。鲁庄公刚要击鼓回应，又被曹刿拦住。

"请通知我方将士坚守阵地，不可出击。"

"Please tell our men to stand firm and hold their ground."

After the army of Qi beat the drums for the third time, Cao Cui said, "Now beat the drums!"

In the ensuing battle, Lu's troops roundly defeated the enemy. Seeing the enemy fleeing, Duke Zhuang was ready to order a chase. Again he was stopped by Cao Gui.

Cao Gui got down from the chariot, walked around to examine the wheel-tracks and hoof-prints of the fleeing enemy and then mounted the chariot to observe their movement.

"All right. We can run after them," he said.

Lu's army pursued the enemy for ten *li*, winning a complete victory.

Duke Zhuang asked Cao Gui to explain his tactics.

"The outcome of a battle," said Cao Gui. "depends on the morale of the soldiers. At the first round of drumbeats, the fighting instinct of the enemy forces was aroused, but we held our ground and did not go forward to meet them. At the second round of drumbeats, the enemy's morale was a little weakened, but was still high. By the time the drums were beat the third time, their enthusiasm had dwindled while the pent-up emotion had made our troops a fierce force. That's why we routed the enemy. Now Qi's army was a formidable one. We must be wary of any possible ambush even when it was retreating. So I got down to take a look at the wheel tracks and hoof-prints. The chaotic condition the enemy left behind, with their banners thrown all over the place, convinced me that it was a genuine retreat. Therefore it was safe to give chase."

178

COMMENT: Seizing the psychological moment to strike at your foe goes a long way toward winning victory.

当齐军擂过第三次鼓后，曹刿才说："现在可以击鼓了。"

结果，齐军被打得落花流水。鲁庄公想要乘胜追击，却被曹刿拦住。曹刿下车观察了齐军留下的车轨痕迹，再上车观察逃跑的敌军后，才说："请主公下令追击。"

鲁国军队追击逃敌十里路，打了一个大胜仗。

鲁庄公请曹刿解释他的策略。

曹刿回答说："打仗靠的是士气。打第一次鼓时，敌军的士气鼓了起来，可是我们按兵不动。打第二次鼓时，敌人的士气削弱了一些，可是依然斗志高昂。打第三次鼓时，敌人的士气已经衰竭，而我们的将士憋了一口气，斗志旺盛，所以能够打败敌军。齐军是劲敌，我们必须提防他们败退时留下埋伏。当我看到齐军车迹混乱，军旗东倒西歪，我知道他们的确是溃败了。所以，追击他们没有危险。"

179

点评：抓住最佳的心理时机打击敌人，对赢得胜利能起很大的作用。

2

TAKE IT EASY

Cao Wei was a distinguished general under Emperor Zhenzong in the Song dynasty. He beat back the enemy many times who marauded China's northwestern border region.

Once the enemy fled after a serious defeat, leaving behind a large number of beasts of burden and other supplies. They were all captured by Cao Wei's army. The animals considerably slowed down the march of his army. Yet General Cao rejected suggestions from his officers that they discard those animals for fear that the enemy might launch a surprise attack.

Soon report came that the enemy was indeed turning back upon learning that the Chinese army was slowed down by their spoils. But General Cao was not concerned at all. He ordered his troops to move on until they reached a favorable terrain. Then he deployed them, waiting for the enemy.

As the enemy troops were drawing near, General Cao dispatched an envoy to their commander, saying that he did not want to attack them when they were tired out but would like to engage them in a battle when they had rested up because he wanted to fight an honest war and win an honest victory. His proposal was readily accepted by the enemy commander whose men had just traveled a hundred *li*.

After a long break, the two sides fought. General Cao's army got the upper hand very soon and crushed the enemy in a

2

礼让败敌

曹玮是宋真宗时的名将。他屡次打败侵犯西北边境的敌人。

有一次，敌人又来骚扰，被曹玮率军打败。敌人溃逃时，丢下许多牛羊和辎重，全被宋军缴获。可是缴获的牛羊使行军的速度大大放慢。部将十分担心敌人偷袭，就建议曹玮扔掉这些牛羊。曹玮只当没有听见。

敌人听说曹玮贪图牛羊，果然掉转马头，进行追袭。曹玮却并不着急。直到军队走到一个有利的地形，才下令停止行军，布阵待敌。

敌人快逼近时，曹玮派使者对敌军将领说："贵军远道而来，想必十分疲劳。我并不想乘你们疲惫不堪的时候进攻。你们可以先休息一下，再开战。我们是仁义之师。胜要胜得光明正大。"

敌军刚跑了将近一百里路。敌军将领欣然接受了他的建议。

等到敌军休息了很长一段时间后，双方交战。没打几个回合，宋军就占了上风，大破敌军。

事后，曹玮告诉部将为什么他能如此轻易获胜的原

big way.

When asked why he was able to win an easy victory, General Cao Wei replied, "Our initial victory did not wipe out the main force of the enemy. So I tried to entice them back by pretending to be greedy and letting those animals hold up the pace of my army. As the enemy troops turned back from a distance, they were naturally tired, but their morale was high. If we fought them right away, there was no guarantee we would win. As we know, if a man stops and takes a rest after a long walk, he'll very likely feel more tired when he gets up. He'll be aching all over and will be in no form to fight. That's why I wanted the enemy to loosen up so that we could defeat them without much difficulty."

COMMENT: Different occasion, different tactics. General Cao Wei's way of winning was just as marvelous as that of Cao Gui.

因。他说："我军起先虽然打败敌人，但并没有消灭他们的有生力量。所以，我装出贪图牛羊的样子来诱敌上钩。敌军远去后又返身追袭，自然十分疲劳。但他们刚靠近我军时，士气还旺盛。如果立刻交战，我军不一定能占上风。大家知道，走远路的人，如果停下来休息后再起身，反而会感到腰酸背痛，打不起精神。所以我让他们先松松劲再交战。这样，我们就能把他们一举击溃。"

点评：曹刿一鼓作气，曹玮礼让败敌，战术不同，却一样聪明。

183

灾 灾
zāi
disaster

此字上部是水，下部是火。水灾和火灾是常见的灾害。
The upper part of the character means water and the lower part a fire. Floods and fire are common disasters.

3

STOP ORDER

Di Qing was a famous general under Emperor Renzong in the Song dynasty. Once his army pursued the enemy forces to the foot of a mountain after a victorious battle. Suddenly the enemy pressed closely together and stopped running. Di Qing ordered his troops to halt even though the soldiers wanted to charge forward. In the end, the enemy got away.

It turned out there was a deep valley on the other side of the mountain. Di Qing's men regretted that they did not continue their pursuit.

"No, it wouldn't be the wise thing to do," said Di Qing. "If a fleeing enemy suddenly stopped and turned around to confront us, it could be a trick. We had already scored a major victory. We could afford to let go the remaining enemy. If we had run after them, we might have fallen into their trap. Then it would be hard to tell the fate of our troops. I would rather that we regret we did not pursue them than we regret we did not stop."

Di Qing's main objective in war was to win victory, not to push the enemy to the limit for some extra gain. He had won many battles but never suffered a major defeat because he was neither greedy nor arrogant when he was victorious.

COMMENT: It is hard to stop when you are victorious. But gain often turns into loss because you don't know where to stop.

3

狄青用兵

　　狄青是宋仁宗时的名将。有一次，他打了一个大胜仗。他的军队追击敌人到一座山脚下时，敌人突然挤成一团，停下来不再跑了。尽管将士们都想追击，狄青却下令收兵。结果敌人得以逃脱。原来，山的那一边是一条深涧。将士们都懊悔莫及。

185

　　狄青却说："追是错误的。逃跑中的敌人突然停下来要跟我们拼命，我怎么知道这不是一个圈套呢？我们已经打了大胜仗，放过残敌也无妨。但是，万一落入他们的圈套，大家是死是活，就不好说了。所以，我宁可后悔没有追击，却不能后悔没有及时收兵。"

　　狄青用兵只求打胜，不求奇功。他之所以打了很多胜仗，而不曾打过大败仗，就是因为在胜利面前，他能够戒骄戒贪。

点评：在胜利的时候停下来是很难的。但是，你往往会因为不知道停止而转胜为败。

4

GENERAL HUO

Six students were on their way to the capital to sit for the imperial examination. When walking along the banks of River Bian one evening, they were surrounded by a dozen bandits. Among the students was a tall and strong man named Huo. He was very good at martial art and had a nickname General Huo.

Huo asked his companions not to panic but stay where they were. Wielding a cudgel in his hand, he confronted the bandits by himself, hitting them mercilessly. Soon everyone of the bandits was knocked to the ground, their legs broken.

The students reported what had happened to the nearest police station which was ten *li* away. When the police arrived at the scene, the bandits were still lying on the ground, groaning from pain.

Huo's fellow students were extremely grateful to him. "If it was not for you," they said. "we would have been in big trouble."

"Not at all," Huo replied. "If I were alone, I might not have won. You see, with all of you standing behind me, I needn't worry about my back. Even though you didn't fight, your presence boosted my courage. That's why I was able to beat them."

COMMENT: General Huo lived up to his nickname. The decisiveness, courage, skill and modesty he demonstrated pointed to the potentials of a good general.

4

霍 将 军

六个学生一起前往京城参加科举考试。一天晚上，他们走在汴河堤上，突然遭遇到一伙盗匪。同行中霍秀才身强力壮，精通武术，外号霍将军。

他叫众人不要逃开，而站在他身后。他一个人挥起一根短棍，迎战盗匪。霍秀才连连奋击，把盗匪一个个打倒在地，打断了腿，不能起来。

众人走了十余里路，将此案报告给了巡警。当巡警赶到现场时，盗匪仍然躺在地上呻吟。

霍秀才的同行非常感激他："如果不是你，我们已经落在盗匪手中了。"

霍秀才说："不能这么说。如果我一个人，未必能打胜。你们站在我的身后，使我没有后顾之忧。你们虽不出力，但给我鼓励，所以我能够打败他们。"

点评：霍将军没有辜负他的外号。他所表现出来的决断、勇气、斗技和谦逊说明他有做一个优秀将领的潜质。

5

ECONOMIC WEAPON

Duke Huan, the ruler of Qi, consulted with his prime minister, Guan Zhong, on how to conquer two of Qi's neighboring states, Lu and Liang.

Guan Zhong said, "Both Lu and Liang are producers of brocade. I suggest that Your Highness put on clothes made of brocade and instruct all government officials to do the same. The people of Qi will likely follow suit. At the same time, you issue a decree to stop all domestic production of brocade. As a result, brocade must be imported from Lu and Liang."

Duke Huan began wearing a brocade robe in public. Meantime, Guan Zhong placed a large order for the fabric with the merchants of Lu and Liang. He told them that Qi would pay three thousand ounces of gold for every thousand bolts of brocade to meet popular demand.

Elated, the rulers of Lu and Liang urged their people to devote themselves to making brocade.

Thirteen months later, Guan Zhong learned that the people of Lu and Liang were so busy making brocade that they had neglected farming. There was an endless line of wagons transporting brocade to Qi.

"Now it is time to conquer them," Guan Zhong told the duke.

"How?"

5

管仲轻重术

齐桓公问相国管仲如何攻克鲁国和梁国。

管仲说:"鲁梁两国擅长织绨。我建议主公穿绨制的衣服,并下令左右大臣也穿绨衣。这样一来,齐国的老百姓就会效仿。同时,下令齐国人不得织绨,所有的绨料都从鲁梁两国进口。"

齐桓公于是在公开场合穿戴绨制的衣服。同时,管仲向鲁梁的商人下了一大张购买绨料的定单。管仲告诉他们,每千匹绨齐国愿意以黄金三千两购买,以满足齐人的需要。

鲁梁两国的君主高兴极了,就鼓励老百姓织绨。

十三个月后,管仲获悉鲁梁两国的人忙于织绨,连耕田都顾不上了。向齐国运绨的货车一辆接一辆,望不到尽头。

管仲告诉齐桓公:"现在可以攻克这两个国家了。"

"如何攻克?"

"请主公在公开场合不再穿绨服而改穿帛衣。同时,封闭关卡,断绝与鲁梁的来往。"

鲁梁两国都不产帛。十个月后,管仲了解到两国的

"Please stop wearing anything made of brocade and change to clothes made of fine silk instead. At the same time, close the borders and cut off the traffic with Lu and Liang."

Neither Lu nor Liang made fine silk. Ten months later, Guan Zhong learned that the people in Lu and Liang were starving; the governments had no revenue. As grain could not be produced in a short time, its price in both states shot up to ten times that in Qi. Soon the economy of the two neighbors collapsed.

In two years, sixty percent of the population in Lu and Liang emigrated to Qi. At the end of another year, the rulers of Lu and Liang were compelled to subject themselves to the rule of Qi.

190

COMMENT: By making their economy totally dependent on exporting to Qi, Lu and Liang courted their own doom.

老百姓都在挨饿，政府没有收入。但是粮食不可能在短时期内生产出来。鲁梁的米价涨到齐国的十倍。两国的经济没多久就崩溃了。

两年后，鲁梁两国的老百姓有百分之六十移居齐国。又过了一年，两国的国君被迫向齐国投降。

点评：鲁梁两国使经济完全依靠向齐国出口，终于自取灭亡。

191

光
guāng
light; glory

此字上部是火，下部是一个跪着的人，表示火给人带来光明。

The pictograph shows a kneeling man with a fire above his head. It conveys the idea that fire brings light to man.

6

CATTLE DEALER

In 627 B.C., the army of Qin approached the state of Zheng in stealth, planning to launch a surprise attack. Xian Gao, a cattle dealer from Zheng, heard the news while he was on his way to sell a herd of cattle near the border.

He was greatly alarmed because the ruler of Zheng had just died and the country was not prepared for war at all. To save his country from the impending disaster, Xian Gao came up with an idea. He picked twelve cattle, dressed up and went to the camp of Qin's troops.

"I am sent by Duke Mu, the new ruler of Zheng, to greet you," he told the commander of the Qin army. "He heard that you are coming to our country, and bade me to bring these cattle to you as gift. They might provide a good meal for your men."

The Qin commander was taken by surprise. This visitor was as much as telling him that Zheng was prepared. He had planned for a quick victory, but it would be impossible now.

"No, no, we are not coming to your country," he told Xian Gao.

Xian Gao looked incredulous.

"We are here because we've lost our way," The general added sheepishly.

After Xian Gao left, the army of Qin made a detour and

6

弦高犒军

公元前 627 年，秦军企图偷袭郑国。郑国牛贩子弦高正赶着一大群牛准备到边地去卖。听到消息后，他大吃一惊，因为郑国国君刚死，毫无打仗准备。

弦高急中生智。他挑了十二头牛，扮作使臣，来到秦军营。

弦高对秦军主帅说："敝国的新君派下臣来远道相迎。他听说贵军来，特使下臣以肥牛十二头作犒师之资，慰劳贵军，给将士们吃一顿。"

秦军主帅十分吃惊。弦高一席话明明是告诉他郑国已经有准备。他原打算速战速决，现在不可能了。

于是，他告诉弦高说："我军到这里来跟郑国没有关系。我们不是往贵国去的。"

炎 yàn blaze; flame	此字由两个"火"组成，其意自明。 As one fire is on top of the other, the meaning of this character is self-evident.

attacked the state of Hua instead.

COMMENT: This was a fine example of subduing the enemy without a fight—the best of all victories. But Xian Gao would not have prevailed if he was not backed by the strength of Zheng.

弦高似乎有点不信。

秦军主帅不好意思地对他说:"我军实在是走迷了路。"

弦高留下了牛走了。秦军于是调转头去攻打滑国。

点评:这是不战而屈人之兵的一个典范。但弦高的外交是以郑国的实力为后盾的。如果没有实力,只有外交,纵使弭患一时,终难避免战乱。

195

工
gōng
work; labor

此字原指古代工匠用的尺,引申为工人、工作。
The character depicts a ruler or a square used by ancient workmen.
It came to mean work or labor.

7

THE SMART ONE

After crossing the Yangtze River, the king of Wu and his hunting party climbed a mountain inhabited by monkeys.

Knowing their lives were in danger, the monkeys all fled into the forest. But there was one monkey who thought he could outsmart the hunters. Swinging from one tree to another nonchalantly, he made a show of his dexterity. The king of Wu raised his bow and shot at him. The monkey nimbly swerved and caught the arrow with his hand.

Annoyed, the king ordered his men to shoot all at once. Unable to dodge the coming arrows, the monkey was killed; his body, bristling with arrows, was nailed to a tree trunk.

The king said to his followers, "The monkey was killed because he was arrogant. He tried to show how clever he was, but he was not really smart. Take this as a lesson."

COMMENT: There is only one step between smartness and stupidity.

7

聪明反被聪明误

吴王打猎的队伍渡过长江，登上猕猴聚居的山岭。

猴子看见了，惊惶四逃，躲进了丛林的深处。只有一只猴子留了下来。它从容不迫地腾身跃起，抓住树枝，跳来跳去，在吴王面前显示它的灵巧。吴王用箭射它，被它敏捷地接住。

吴王发了怒。他下令左右随从一齐射箭。猴子躲避不及，抱树而死。

吴王对他的随从说："这只猴子夸耀它的灵巧，结果被杀死了。它想显示自己有多聪明，但它不是真的聪明。你们要以此为鉴。"

评语：聪明和愚蠢之间只相差一步。

8

SPY AND COUNTERSPY

At the end of the Han dynasty, China entered what is known as the Period of the Three Kingdoms, during which, Wei, Wu and Shu were contending against one another for supremacy.

Cao Cao, the ruler of Wei, dominated the north. Wei was the most powerful of the three. As prime minister of the Han court, Cao Cao used the young emperor as a puppet, in whose name, to issue orders and attack his rivals. Wu controlled the lower reaches of the Yangtze River. Shu, located in modern Sichuan, was the weakest of the three. Faced with the common threat from Wei, Wu and Shu formed an alliance.

In 208, Cao Cao's army of 200,000 was ready to sail down the Yangtze River to invade Wu. But his troops were northerners with little experience in naval warfare. So Cao Cao ordered Zhang Yun and Cai Mao, two officers of the Wu navy who had defected, to train his men.

The training was conducted day and night. Bright torches and glowing water could be seen from the south bank. General Zhou Yu, commander of the Wu army, got on a boat to spy on the enemy. What he saw worried him, because the training was very professional.

It happened that his former fellow student, Jiang Gan, came to visit him. Jiang Gan was Cao Cao's advisor, but denied he came as Cao Cao's envoy.

8

将计就计

东汉末年，中国进入三国时期，魏吴蜀争夺天下。魏国霸据中国北方，势力最大。魏主曹操是朝廷丞相。他挟天子以令诸侯，皇帝成了他手中的傀儡。吴国控制长江中下游地区。位于四川省的蜀国最弱。吴蜀两国为了对抗共同的威胁，结成了联盟。

公元 208 年，曹操率领二十万大军沿长江南下准备灭吴。可是，他的士兵大半是北方人，不习水战。于是，曹操起用两名吴国水军的降官蔡瑁和张允训练水军，夜以继日，晚上灯火照得水面通红。吴军统帅周瑜亲自乘船窥探后，大吃一惊，因为两名军官的训练深得水军之妙。

恰巧，他的昔日同窗蒋干来访。蒋干是曹操的谋士，周瑜问他是不是为曹操做说客来的。蒋干矢口否认。周瑜把蒋干介绍给部下相见，并大摆宴席招待他。席间，周瑜兴致勃勃，还舞了一回剑。

深夜散席时，周瑜已经大醉。他把蒋干带到自己的寝室，提议两人像学生时代一样同寝一室。周瑜倒头就睡，可是蒋干睡不着。他看见桌上放着一堆文书，就起床偷看，原来都是书信。其中一封信有蔡瑁、张允的签名。

Zhou Yu held a dinner party in his honor attended by many of his officers. The party went on till late into night. Zhou Yu seemed in high spirits. He even performed a sword dance for his friend. By the time the party was over, Zhou Yu was quite drunk.

He took Jiang Gan to his bedroom and suggested they share the room as they used to in their student days. Then he flung himself onto the bed and immediately fell asleep.

But Jiang Gan could not sleep. Looking around, he saw a pile of papers on the desk. They were letters. One bearing the signatures of Generals Cai Mao and Zhang Yun caught his eye. It said that they did not surrender to Cao Cao willingly, but were driven to do so by circumstances. That they were not really training his navy, but trapping them in the naval camps. And they promised to get in touch with Zhou Yu again.

Good gracious! Jiang Gan grabbed the letter and hid it in his clothes. In the middle of the night, he heard somebody coming to wake up Zhou Yu. He pretended to be asleep, but strained his ears trying to catch Zhou Yu's conversation outside. He vaguely heard the names of Cai Mao and Zhang Yun being mentioned.

The next morning Jiang Gan left Wu while Zhou Yu was still sleeping. As soon as he returned, he showed the letter to Cao Cao. Cao Cao was thrown into a rage. He immediately ordered the two officers to be beheaded. But as soon as they were dead, he realized he had been tricked. When other officers asked him for the reason, Cao Cao, ever so loath to admit his own mistakes, replied, "They were executed because they lacked discipline."

COMMENT: If Jiang Gan had asked himself why such confidential information could find its way into his hands so easily, he might not have walked into Zhou Yu's trap.

信上说，他们是不得已才投降曹操的。他们并不想训练曹操的水军，而是想把曹军困在水寨里。

蒋干大吃一惊，就把信暗藏在衣内。半夜里，他听见有人入内叫醒周瑜。蒋干只装睡着，却窃听外面的谈话。虽然听不清内容，但听见周瑜提到张、蔡两人的名字。

第二天清晨，周瑜还没有起来，蒋干就告辞了。他回去后，将信交给曹操。曹操大怒，立刻将张、蔡两人斩首。可是刚一斩首，就醒悟到他中了周瑜的计。当部下问他为何杀死张、蔡两人时，曹操不肯认错，只好说两人怠慢军法，所以斩首。

201

点评：如果蒋干问问自己，如此重要的机密文件为什么能够如此轻易到手，他也许就不至于上当了。

力
lì
power;
strength

此字原像古代的犁，说明耕田需用力。
The original pictograph depicted an ancient plough. It tells us ploughing requires strength.

9

ARROW PROCUREMENT

At that time, Zhuge Liang, Shu's chief strategist, was staying in Wu to work on a common strategy against Cao Cao. When Lu Su, Zhou Yu's advisor, visited him, Zhuge congratulated him on Zhou Yu's success in getting rid of the two southern generals with a ruse.

"Zhou Yu can only fool Jiang Gan," said Zhuge. "but not Cao Cao. Cao Cao must have realized his mistake by now. However, he wouldn't admit it."

Although Lu Su promised Zhuge not to say anything to Zhou Yu, he reported Zhuge's remarks to Zhou Yu, anyway. Zhou Yu was troubled that Zhuge could read his mind. He was jealous of Zhuge who was said to be a man of extraordinary talent. Zhou Yu decided to find a way to embarrass Zhuge.

The following morning he invited Zhuge to a meeting with his officers.

"What weapon is the most effective in a naval battle?" he asked Zhuge.

"Arrows are the best," answered Zhuge.

"True. However, our supplies are running short. Could you help us replenish them? We'll need 100,000 arrows for the forthcoming battle. I hope you won't refuse."

"I'll certainly do my best, General," said Zhuge. "When do you need them?"

9

草船借箭

　　周瑜用计除掉了替曹操训练水军的两个将官后，他的谋士鲁肃造访了正在吴国的蜀国军师诸葛亮。诸葛亮是来跟周瑜共商抗曹大计的。

　　诸葛亮向鲁肃道喜。他说："周瑜的这条计谋，只好骗蒋干。曹操虽然一时被瞒过，但一定会醒悟，只是不会认错罢了。"

　　尽管诸葛亮吩咐鲁肃不要对周瑜传话，但鲁肃还是将诸葛亮的话向周瑜报告了。周瑜对诸葛亮识破他的计谋深感不安。他早就听说诸葛亮才识过人，因此心怀妒忌，决定找个机会使诸葛亮难堪。

　　第二天，他召集众将开会，请诸葛亮出席。

　　周瑜问诸葛亮："若打水仗，什么兵器最重要？"

　　诸葛亮说："弓箭最佳。"

　　周瑜说："我同意。但现在军中正缺箭用。敢烦先生监制十万支箭供备战用。希望先生不要推却。"

　　诸葛亮说："我自当效劳，请问将军何时要用箭？"

　　"十天之内可以办完吗？"

　　"十天太长了，敌人随时会来。"

"Can you make it in ten days?"

"Ten days would be too long. The enemy may come at any time."

"How much time do you need?"

"I'll have them ready in three days."

"There is no joking in the army, sir."

"How dare I joke with you, General? If I can't deliver them in time, I am willing to accept punishment. I am willing to give you a written guarantee. I'll start tomorrow. Three days from tomorrow, you will please send five hundred men to the riverside to collect the arrows."

Zhou Yu was greatly pleased that Zhuge offered to sign a written guarantee, but secretly ordered materials for making arrows to be withheld and the workmen to go slow. Then he sent Lu Su to find out what Zhuge was doing.

Zhuge blamed Lu Su for not keeping his word and asked him to help him out.

"You brought trouble on yourself," said Lu Su. "How can I help you?"

"You can. I would like to borrow twenty boats. On each boat please install at least fifty jacks of straw covered by black cloth and line them up on both sides of each boat, and I need thirty men for each boat. But you must not let General Zhou Yu know, or my plan will fail."

Though puzzled, Lu Su obliged Zhuge. The vessels were prepared without Zhou Yu's knowledge. Zhuge did nothing for two days. Then on the third day, he secretly called upon Lu Su before daybreak.

"Come to my boat with me. We're going to collect the arrows."

"先生需要几天办完呢？"

"我三天就可以办完。"

"军中无戏言。"

"我怎么敢戏弄将军呢？三天办不好，我甘愿受罚。我甘愿立下军令状。从明天起开始造，请你第三天派五百名士兵到江边搬箭。"

周瑜很高兴，让诸葛亮立了军令状。同时，他命令工匠故意延迟，造箭的原料也不给齐。然后，他命鲁肃去探听虚实。

诸葛亮责备鲁肃没有遵守诺言。他请鲁肃帮忙。

鲁肃说："你自取其祸，我怎么帮得了你呢？"

诸葛亮说："你帮得了。我想借二十条船。每条船上需要军士三十人。船上用青布为幔。至少立五十个稻草人分布两边。不过，不能让周瑜知道，否则，我的计划就会失败。"

鲁肃虽然不解，还是照办了。他没有向周瑜提起借船的事。第一、第二天不见诸葛亮有任何动静。第三天黎明时分，诸葛亮密访鲁肃。

"请到我船中来，我们一起去取箭。"

"到哪里去取？"

"不要多问，去了就知道。"

二十条船用长索相连，径往北岸进发。那时大雾漫天，对面不见人。当船靠近曹军水寨时，诸葛亮命令士

"Where are we going?"

"You'll know soon."

The twenty vessels, fastened together with long ropes, set out for the northern shore in a dense fog. Visibility was reduced to a few feet. As the vessels came in view of Cao Cao's camp, Zhuge ordered the crew to beat drums and shout battle cries.

Lu Su was alarmed. "What if the enemy comes out?"

Zhuge laughed. "I'd be surprised if Cao Cao would venture out in this weather. Let's have a drink. We'll return when the fog disappears."

Cao Cao, suspecting an ambush, ordered his men to shoot arrows to prevent the enemy from landing, and dispatched a reinforcement of six thousand to the river bank. Zhuge ordered the boats to turn around and get closer to the shore to take more arrow shots while the crew on the boats kept beating the drums and shouting battle cries. Arrows fell on the boats like rain.

When the sun rose and the fog began to lift, Zhuge ordered the boats to speed back home. Seeing the straw jacks on the boats bristling with arrows, he ordered the crew to shout, "Thank you for your arrows, Prime Minister!"

By the time Cao Cao realized what had happened, Zhuge's boats were beyond overtaking.

"You are a genius," said Lu Su. "How did you know there would be a fog today?"

"A general who is ignorant of astronomy and geography," Zhuge replied. "will never rise above mediocrity. I knew three days ago there would be a heavy fog this morning. That's why I took a chance. Zhou Yu offered me ten days but withheld labor and raw materials. Obviously he did not want me to succeed so

兵击鼓呐喊。

鲁肃惊呼："如果曹兵出来打我们怎么办？"

诸葛亮笑着说："曹操在这种天气一定不敢出来。我们只管饮酒，等雾散了就回去。"

曹操听到擂鼓呐喊声，推想重雾之中敌军必有埋伏，就传令士兵放箭，力阻敌军登陆。又从别处增派六千名弓弩手到江边助射。诸葛亮把船头掉转，逼近水寨受箭。同时，军士们不停地擂鼓呐喊。曹军的箭如雨一般落在船上。

到日高雾散时，诸葛亮命令收船急回。二十条船的稻草人身上插满了箭支。诸葛亮命令船上的军士齐声喊叫："谢丞相箭。"

等曹操得知后，诸葛亮已经船轻水急，追之不及。

鲁肃敬佩地对诸葛亮说："先生真是神人，何以知道今天有如此大雾呢？"

207

口
kǒu
mouth

一张张大的嘴。
The pictograph of an open mouth.

that he could punish me. But how can he harm me as my fate is linked with Heaven?"

On the south shore five hundred soldiers were waiting to collect the arrows. The final count exceeded 150,000.

COMMENT: Zhuge Liang (181–234) was twenty-eight at the time. Later he was appointed prime minister of Shu and won many battles. Regarded as the most brilliant strategist and tactician in history, Zhuge Liang's name is a household word in China, synonymous with wisdom and resourcefulness.

诸葛亮回答说："为将而不通天文、不识地理，就是庸才。我三天前已经算定今天有大雾，因此敢冒这次险。周瑜叫我十天办完，却不给我工匠、材料，他分明是要惩罚我。可是我的命和天连在一起，他怎么能害我呢？"

在南岸江边，五百名士兵正等待取箭。所得总计超过十五万支。

点评：当时诸葛亮年仅二十八岁。他后来担任蜀国的丞相，打过许多胜仗，是中国历史上最杰出的战略家和战术家。诸葛亮在中国家喻户晓，他的名字成了足智多谋、神机妙算的代名词。

加
jiā
add; increase

此字将力和口结合在一起，意为"增加"。
The left side of this ideograph means strength and the right side mouth. When words are backed by force, your talk is more effective. Hence the meaning.

10

SELF-SACRIFICE

Cao Cao's army of 200,000 was stationed on the north bank of the Yangtze. The combined forces of Wu and Shu were only 50,000. General Zhou Yu decided the best way of breaking the enemy was to launch a fire attack. But a fire attack would be effective only if his army was able to get close to the enemy.

Zhou Yu was pondering what to do when two cousins of Cai Mao, the former Wu officer executed by Cao Cao, came over and surrendered themselves. Zhou Yu had an idea. He welcomed the two men, rewarded them and let them stay in the army camp. That night he summoned an old general named Huang Gai for a confidential conversation.

At a meeting with his officers the following day, Zhou Yu said that they should prepare for a three-month hold-out with Cao Cao. But he was opposed by Huang Gai.

"Three months? What good is it even if we can hold out for thirty months? If we can't win in a month, we might as well surrender to Cao Cao."

Zhou Yu was enraged. "Our mission is to defeat Cao Cao," he snarled. "How dare you talk about surrender?"

A heated argument followed and Zhou Yu ordered Huang Gai to be dragged out. Huang Gai became abusive. Zhou Yu was so provoked he ordered Huang Gai to be summarily executed. Many officers came forward to plead in behalf of

10

苦 肉 计

曹操有二十万大军驻扎在长江北岸，而吴蜀联军加起来只有五万人。吴军统帅周瑜认为最好的攻敌策略是火攻。可是，用火攻必须接近敌军才能实现。

周瑜正为此事苦恼，忽报被曹操处决的吴军军官蔡瑁的两个族弟前来投降。周瑜心生一计。他热情地接待了两人，让他们留在军中。当晚，他召见老将黄盖作了一次密谈。

第二天，周瑜召集诸将开会。会上，他要大家做好三个月的御敌准备。

话音未落，黄盖就表示反对。他说："莫说三个月，就是三十个月，也无济于事。如果我们一个月内不能破敌，还不如投降曹操更好。"

周瑜大怒："我们的任务是打败曹操，你怎么敢说投降？"

他下令将黄盖赶出去。黄盖破口大骂，周瑜更加生气，下令将他斩首。黄盖是一名劳苦功高、忠心耿耿的老将。众将官苦苦哀求，周瑜才饶了他一命，但将他打

Huang Gai who had served the country with utter devotion for many years. In the end Huang Gai was given fifty lashes. The beating was so severe that Huang Gai lost consciousness.

A few days later, a man claiming to be a friend of General Huang Gai's brought Cao Cao a letter from Huang Gai in which he complained about his treatment under Zhou Yu and stated his intention to defect. He promised to bring over with him ships and equipment. Cao Cao was suspicious. It was not until he received a letter from the cousins of Cai Mao, who had been sent to Wu to collect intelligence, confirming the beating of General Huang Gai, that he was convinced.

On the eve of the winter solstice, a message from Huang Gai informed Cao Cao that he had been assigned to escort a shipment of grain and would direct the convoy to Cao Cao's camp at midnight. Overjoyed, Cao Cao went aboard a large ship and stayed up waiting for him.

At midnight, an easterly wind rose. At about the same time, Huang Gai's fleet appeared in the distance. As the ships drew nearer, Cao Cao became suspicious. Why were the ships moving so fast if they were loaded with grain?

In fact Huang Gai had prepared twenty ships loaded with combustibles, their prows studded with giant nails, their inside stacked with reeds and straws soaked in fish oil and overspread with sulfur and saltpeter. All were covered with black cloth.

Before Cao Cao could stop him, Huang Gai set the first row of his vessels on fire. Sped by the wind, the vessels dashed toward Cao Cao's fleet like flying arrows. Cao Cao's boats were chained together. When one caught fire, others could not flee. Tongues of fire rose; the sky was lit up. Huang Gai's burning ships closed in from all sides. Cao Cao's naval camp was turned

了五十脊杖。黄盖被打得皮开肉绽，昏死过去。

几天以后，一个自称为黄盖的朋友的人来见曹操，把黄盖的一封信交给他。信中黄盖表示因无罪受刑，心里痛恨周瑜，愿率粮草船只投降曹操。曹操将信将疑，直到来自蔡瑁的族弟的密书确认黄盖受刑的消息后，才信以为真。

冬至前夜，黄盖来信称，周瑜派他运送新到的粮草。他准备在当天半夜带船队前来投降。曹操大喜，就登上一艘大船等候。

那天半夜，忽然刮起了东南风。当黄盖的船队走近时，曹操起了疑心。粮在船中，船必稳重，为什么来船走得这么快？

213

原来黄盖的二十条船装的都是易燃物。船头密布大钉，内装芦苇干柴，灌以鱼油，上铺硫磺焰硝引火之物，全用青布遮盖。

曹操来不及阻挡，黄盖就把第一排船点燃。火乘风势，船如箭发，撞向曹军水寨。曹操的船只被铁环锁住，一艘起火，别的也无法逃脱。黄盖的火船把曹军水寨包围。风助火势，一瞬间，整个水寨变成一片火海。烈火又从水上蔓延到陆地，将曹操的陆上军营也吞噬了。

在吴蜀联军的攻击下，曹军遭到了摧毁性的打击。

周瑜从一开始就知道，蔡瑁族弟的投降是一个骗局，因为他们没有把自己的家眷带来。周瑜利用他们

into a raging inferno. His tents on land also caught fire. His entire army was thrown into a pandemonium. Under the attack of the joint forces of Wu and Shu, Cao Cao's army suffered a devastating defeat.

Zhou Yu knew from the beginning that the defection of Cai Mao's cousins was a hoax since they did not bring their families with them. He used them to pass misinformation to Cao Cao, which contributed to the victory of what is known as the Battle of the Red Cliff, one of the most famous battles in Chinese history.

214

COMMENT: This is an example of the ruse of inflicting injury upon oneself so as to mislead the enemy and cause them to suffer a greater loss.

向曹操传达错误的信息，从而促成了中国历史上最有
名的战役——赤壁大战的胜利。

点评：这是一种苦肉计，是自愿使自己受损，以误导敌人，使他蒙受更大损
失的一种策略。

甘
gān
sweet

此字画的是口里咬着一样东西，那东西的味道一定美。
The pictograph depicts something inside the mouth. It must taste
good. Hence its meaning.

11

EAST WIND

Had his vessels not been fastened together, Cao Cao would not have sustained such heavy losses. As a matter of fact, the idea of fastening his vessels was given him by a spy from Wu. At the time his soldiers were ill because they were not used to living on the water. The spy suggested that all the vessels be fastened with iron chains in groups and covered with planks. This way men and horses could walk from boat to boat as if they were walking on dry land without fear of rough waves and winds. Cao Cao thought it was a great idea.

One of his advisors objected. "Chaining the boats together will make them steady. But if the enemy attacks us by fire, we will be in deep trouble."

Cao Cao laughed. "Good thinking! But you overlooked one thing. A fire attack must depend on the direction of the wind. We are in the middle of winter. The wind only blows from the north or the west, not from the south or the east. If the enemy uses fire, they will only burn themselves out."

It never occurred to him that there could be an easterly wind in the middle of winter.

The issue of the wind had been very much on Zhou Yu's mind too, for a fire attack could not succeed without an east wind. Earlier, he was so anxious that he fell ill. When Zhuge Liang called on him, he told Zhou Yu he knew what was

11

借 东 风

如果曹军的战船没有锁在一起，曹操本来不会在赤壁大战中遭到如此惨败。连环计其实是周瑜的间谍向曹操献的计。那时曹军因水土不服，许多人生了病。周瑜的间谍提议用铁环将大小船只连锁在一起，上面铺上阔板，任凭风浪潮水，人和马都可以在上面如履平地。

曹操认为这是一个妙策。但是，他的一名谋士提出异议。

"船都连锁固然平稳，但如果敌人用火攻，我们就麻烦了。"

曹操笑道："你虽有远虑，但是忽略了一件事。凡用火攻，必借风力。如今隆冬之际，只有西风北风，没有东风南风。我们在西北，对方在南岸。如果他用火攻，是烧自己的兵，我有什么可怕呢？"

曹操万万没有想到此时会有东风。

其实，周瑜也没有想到。没有东风，火攻不可能成功。为了此事，周瑜郁闷得生了病。诸葛亮探病时告诉他，他知道周瑜生的是什么病，并写了一个药方给

bothering him and wrote a prescription for Zhou Yu.

To break Cao Cao,
We must use fire.
Now we've got everything except the east wind.

Zhou Yu was shocked. "What cure do you have?"

"I happen to know how to call up winds by praying to Heaven. I'll need an altar on Mount Nanping for the purpose. I'll go there and pray for a strong southeast wind to rise and blow for three days and three nights."

"One night would be sufficient." Zhou Yu's spirits were restored.

An altar was built on Mount Nanping according to Zhuge's specifications. Zhuge went there to pray the day before the winter solstice. Just as he had promised, a strong southeasterly wind rose around midnight.

Now that victory over Cao Cao was virtually assured, Zhou Yu decided it was time to get rid of Zhuge whom he had always regarded as a potential threat to Wu. He dispatched a hundred men to Mount Nanping to capture him, but Zhuge was nowhere to be found. A search by land and water ensued.

But Zhuge was already sailing away in a boat escorted by Shu's most valiant general, Zhao Yun.

"It's no use chasing me," Zhuge shouted to his pursuers. "I know what Zhou Yu is up to. I can read his mind like a book. I'm going home now."

Twang! General Zhao Yun shot down the sail of the pursuing boat and Zhuge's boat sped away.

周瑜看。

"欲破曹操，宜用火攻，万事齐备，只欠东风。"

周瑜见了大惊。"先生将用什么药治我的病呢？"

诸葛亮说："我学过呼风唤雨的本事。只要在南屏山上建一台，我愿上台作法，借三天三夜的东南大风，助你用兵。"

周瑜精神顿起。"只要一夜大风就成了。"

于是，他在南屏山上按诸葛亮的要求筑了七星坛。诸葛亮在冬至前夜登坛作法。果然在三更时分，东南风大起。

风一起，周瑜知道赤壁之战已稳操胜券。但诸葛亮此人不可留，必须及早除掉，以免他日成为吴国祸根。于是他派遣了一百名将士前往南屏山捉拿诸葛亮。可是南屏山上已不见诸葛亮踪影。周瑜立即兵分水陆两路搜寻追袭。

此时，诸葛亮已由蜀国有万夫不当之勇的赵云将军坐船接走。

诸葛亮对追船上的人说："你们不必追了。我料定周瑜不能容我，必来加害，所以我现在回去了。"

赵云拈弓搭箭，射断了追船上的帆，然后疾驶而去，吴兵追之不及。

219

COMMENT: The ostensible reason Zhuge Liang went to Mount Nanping was to pray for easterly winds. But his real purpose was to escape. Zhuge had lived in the area for a long time and knew that the winter solstice usually brought about a change of winds.

He had been under the watchful eyes of Zhou Yu since he came to Wu and was well aware of Zhou Yu's intention. To pray for easterly winds was a perfect reason to ascend Mount Nanping, which gave him the chance to get away. By achieving his rival's objective, he achieved his own.

点评：诸葛亮去南屏山的表面原因是借东风，但实际目的是逃跑。诸葛亮在当地住了很长时间，知道冬至期间风向会变。自从他来吴之后，一直受到周瑜的监督，有性命之虞。去南屏山借东风，给了他一个逃脱的机会。

诸葛亮通过实现对手的目的，实现了自己的目的。

去
qù
go; leave

此字上部原是人，下部原是口，表示人从洞穴口出去。因为古代的人住在洞穴里。

The upper part of pictograph was originally a man and the lower part a mouth, meaning a man leaving the mouth of his cave. Men used to live in caves in ancient times.

12

THE HUARONG TRAIL

As Cao Cao and his men fled the battlefield of the Red Cliff, they were ambushed twice by Zhuge Liang until their number was reduced to a few hundred. Hungry and exhausted, Cao Cao decided to return to his stronghold, Xuchang, in Henan.

"Which is the shorter route to our destination?" Cao Cao asked his officers as they came to a crossroads after clearing out a burning forest.

"The highway is smooth, but it would be time-consuming to take it. The Huarong Trail is a shortcut but it is rough and narrow."

Smoke could be seen along the Huarong Trail but the highway was quiet. Cao Cao decided to take the shortcut.

His officers objected. "But there is smoke. There may be troops in ambush."

"No," said Cao Cao. "One should never trust appearances in fighting. Zhuge Liang has lit the fire so that we dare not go that way. I'm sure he has laid an ambush on the highway. I won't fall into his trap."

The Huarong Trail was muddy, narrow, and full of potholes. Horses were bogged down in the mire. The soldiers had to throw away much of their equipment to be able to walk. They had to repair the road as they trudged along. After

12

华 容 道

曹操的军马从赤壁战场逃出来，又两次遭到诸葛亮的伏兵打击，最后只剩下几百人马。曹操人饥马困，决定返回守地河南许昌。

曹军走到一个路口，前面有两条路。曹操问军士："哪条路近？"

军士回答："大路平坦，但远一些。小路华容道近，只是地窄路险。"

曹操看见华容道上有几处烟起，大路则没有动静，就决定走小路。

将士们都不同意。"风烟起处，必有埋伏。"

曹操说："兵书上说，虚则实之，实则虚之。诸葛亮故意叫人在华容道上烧烟，使我们不敢走。我料定他的伏兵在大路上等着，我偏不中他的计。"

华容道泥泞不堪，马蹄陷在泥里，不能前行。士兵们抛弃装备，才能行走。他们一边修路，一边前进。好不容易走过了一段险峻之路后，曹操忽然大笑起来。

"诸葛亮如果真是聪明的话，在这里设埋伏，我们就只好束手就擒了。"

crossing a particularly difficult section of the trail, Cao Cao broke into a laugh.

"If Zhuge Liang were smart, he would have us sniped here."

Barely had he finished speaking when hundreds of swordsmen of the Shu army appeared on both side of the trail. At the sight of the enemy, Cao Cao's men were frightened out of their wits. They had lost their will to fight. Cao Cao thought he was doomed.

Fortunately, the Shu general, Guan Yu, had once been his guest and treated with warm hospitality. Cao Cao pleaded for mercy. Guan Yu was a man of honor. Looking at the deplorable condition of Cao Cao and his men, he took pity on them and let them go.

Of Cao Cao's original army of 200,000, only 27 survived the battle of the Red Cliff. As a result, Wei was seriously weakened and a power balance was established among the three kingdoms of Wei, Wu and Shu.

COMMENT: Zhuge Liang outwitted Cao Cao because he knew his way of thinking. Cao Cao was a good strategist and good at deceiving people. The only way to induce him to the Huarong Trail was to let him see the smoke on the trail. When Cao Cao saw the smoke, he would think it was a ruse to divert him away from the trail and would take the trail precisely for that reason.

话音未落，路两旁突然出现数百名蜀军的刀斧手。曹军吓得魂飞魄散，完全丧失了斗志。曹操以为自己命将休矣。

幸亏蜀军将领关羽曾经作过曹操的座上客，受到过曹操的盛情招待。曹操求关羽饶命。关羽是一个讲义气的人，此刻动了恻隐之心，就放过了曹操。

曹操的二十万军马，只有二十七人在赤壁大战中活了下来。魏国因赤壁大战之故被严重削弱。魏、吴、蜀三国形成了鼎立的局面。

225

点评：诸葛亮战胜曹操，是因为他摸透了曹操的思路。曹操是一个相当不错的战略家，常用欺骗手段战胜敌人。诸葛亮明白引诱他走华容道的唯一办法是让他看到华容道上冒烟。曹操会认为这是敌人想诱他回避华容道，因而会偏偏选择华容道。

男
nán
man; male

此字将田和力结合在一起，古时候，下田耕种主要是男子的工作。
The character combines field with power. In ancient times, ploughing the field was a man's job.

13

EMPTY CITY STRATAGEM

Here is another celebrated example of Zhuge Liang's feat. Once he was confronted with an extremely dangerous situation: An enemy battalion 150,000 strong was approaching an isolated city garrisoned by only a handful of old soldiers under his command when his main force was away.

Zhuge ordered all the flags in sight to be taken down and all the city gates thrown open. He had soldiers dressed as scavengers to sweep the streets at the city gates. No one was permitted to move about or make any noise. Then dressed in his usual white robe, he mounted the city wall, lit a stick of incense and began playing a piece of peaceful music on the lute. When the enemy commander saw the scene, he immediately suspected a sinister trap and withdrew. By the time he found out the truth, Shu's main force had already returned.

COMMENT: Zhuge had a reputation for being cautious and risk-averse. Knowing that his opponent was a shrewd man who loved deception in strategy but often fell victim to his own suspicion, he gambled on his suspicion. Acting out of character, Zhuge succeeded in deceiving him.

13

空 城 计

再举一个诸葛亮的用计佳话。

有一次,诸葛亮面临一个极其险恶的情况。一支十五万人的敌军向他驻守的孤城杀来。可是诸葛亮军队的主力不在城中,他身边只有一些老兵。

诸葛亮传令将旌旗收起,城门大开,用军士扮作清道夫在城门口扫街。同时,禁止人们走动及高声言语。

然后,他身披鹤氅,登上城楼,焚香操琴。敌军将领见此情形,怀疑城中有埋伏,就下令退兵。当敌军知道真相后,蜀军主力已经返回。

点评:诸葛亮平生谨慎,从不冒险。他深知对手喜欢用诈,却多猜忌,就利用其疑心,一改惯例,反常用兵,成功地欺骗了对手。

14

IMITATION

After reading about how Zhuge Liang scared off an invading enemy by opening the gates of a defenseless city, a scholar decided to imitate him. Before he went to the theater in the evening, he left the doors of his house wide open and the rooms well-lit. When he returned home that night, he was very pleased that nothing was stolen.

A few days later, before he went out in the evening, he did the same thing again. This time, however, his house was burglarized. Upset, he complained to a friend of his that Zhuge Liang's idea was not so brilliant after all.

"Did Zhuge use his trick twice?" asked his friend.

"No."

"Then why did you use it twice?"

The scholar was dumbfounded.

COMMENT: Don't use the same trick twice.

14

模仿空城计

　　有个书生读了诸葛亮用空城计吓退敌军的故事后，决定模仿他。他晚上出门看戏前，将大门打开，里面点得灯火通明。回来后，发现家中没被盗窃，他很高兴。

　　几天后，他晚上出去，又是如此。这一次他家中被偷窃了。他很不高兴，向朋友抱怨说："诸葛亮的计谋并不怎么高明。"

　　朋友问他："诸葛亮的空城计用过第二次吗？"

　　"没有。"

　　"那么，你为什么要用第二次呢？"

　　书生顿时语塞，无言以对。

点评：同样的计策不宜再用。

15

TWO PURSUITS

General Zhang Xiu was fighting Cao Cao and found him a formidable opponent. When he learned Cao Cao was pulling back his army to rush home, because his capital Xudu was under the attack by another warlord, he decided to launch a hot pursuit and attack Cao Cao's retreating army.

His advisor Jia Xu tried to dissuade him. "Don't do that. If you chase him, you will be defeated."

"But I'm not going to miss this opportunity."

General Zhang Xiu's ten thousand men quickly overtook Cao Cao's rear guard. But Cao Cao's army fought so furiously that they threw back their pursuers.

General Zhang Xiu was filled with regret. "I wish I had heeded your warning," he said to Jia Xu.

"Now you can turn round and pursue Cao Cao again," Jia Xu said.

"But we've just been defeated."

"This time I guarantee you will win."

General Zhang ran after Cao Cao a second time. Just as Jia Xu had predicted, his troops put Cao Cao's army to rout.

"Why is it that the first time we pursued him with our best troops but were defeated and the second time our defeated troops were able to win?"

"You are well-versed in the art of war," explained Jia Xu.

15

二次追曹

张绣将军跟曹操作战，发现曹操很厉害。当他听说曹操因另一个军阀侵犯许都而急忙撤军，就下令追击。

谋士贾诩说："不可以追。如果追的话，一定会被曹军打败。"

张绣说："我不能坐失良机。"

张绣的一万人马很快追上曹军。但是曹军奋战，张绣大败而逃。

张绣后悔不已，对贾诩说："我不听你的劝告，果然败了。"

贾诩说："现在你可以整兵再前往追击。"

张绣说："可是我们刚刚打了败仗呀。"

"这次我保证你打胜仗。"

张绣再次追击，果然打败了曹军。

张绣问："为什么第一次我用精兵追曹军被打败，第二次我用败兵追胜兵，却打了胜仗呢？"

贾诩答道："将军虽然善于用兵，但不是曹操的对手。曹操撤军时，必然有劲旅断后，以防追兵。所以你追兵

"but your opponent is even better. When Cao Cao ordered a retreat, he was bound to leave his best troops in the rear to ward off any attack. Therefore you stood little chance of winning even with your best troops. But Cao Cao was anxious to go back. Once he had beat off your attack, he would not be concerned with the rear defense. This has created an opportunity for you."

General Zhang could not but marvel at Jia Xu's insight.

COMMENT: Jia Xu might be called "a lateral thinker." Most people have an established pattern of reasoning. A lateral thinker is capable of switching his pattern of thinking and looking at things from a different angle.

虽精，也不能打赢。可是曹操急于回去，既然他破了你的追军，就不会再留下后卫，所以你可以乘其不备。"

张绣听后恍然大悟，非常佩服贾诩的高明。

点评：贾诩可称为一个有"侧面思维"的人。多数人的推理遵循固定的模式。侧面思维者能从一个思维模式切换到另外一个模式，从不同的角度观察问题，解决问题。

233

功
gōng
achievement;
merit

此字的左边是工作，右边是力，意思是通过努力工作而获得成就。
The left side of the character means work and the right side strength. Putting them together means achievement.

16

TWO PEACHES AND THREE WARRIORS

There were three brave warriors in Qi: Gongsun Jie, Tian Kaijiang and Gu Yezi. They were arrogant and overbearing in the court. Ministers found them hard to get along with and Duke Jing was irritated by their rudeness. When Prime Minister Yan Ying greeted them, they did not bother to acknowledge him. Yan Ying decided to get rid of them.

"Your Highness," he said to the duke. "The three brave men are getting too proud of themselves. They should be respectful of their ruler and other officials, but their behavior is setting a bad example to their juniors. Such soldiers cannot be relied on to fight for the country. Sooner or later, they'll get out of control."

"But what can we do? They are strong and skilled in fighting. You have no way to get rid of them. Shoot, you will miss. Fight, you will lose."

"They've only got physical strength. That's all."

One day, Duke Zhao, the ruler of Lu, visited Qi. Duke Jing gave a banquet in his honor. After the main course, peaches were served. Peaches were a rare delicacy in Qi. But there were only five on the table. One went to Duke Zhao of Lu, one to Duke Jing who gave the third one to Yan Ying.

Duke Jing let Yan Ying decide who among the three warriors, who were also attending the banquet, would get the remaining two peaches.

"I'll give this peach to one of you who has the greatest

16

二桃杀三士

　　公孙接、田开疆、古冶之是齐国的三个勇士。他们在朝廷横行霸道，旁若无人。大臣们难以和他们相处。齐景公见了他们，如芒刺在背。齐相晏婴问候三人，三人也不回礼。晏婴决心除去这三人。

　　晏婴对景公说："这三个勇士对上没有君臣之道，对下没有长幼之礼。他们为下属树立了一个坏榜样。主公不可能依靠他们攻击敌人。他们迟早会变得无法无天。"

　　齐景公说："可是，我们有什么办法呢？这三人勇敢过人，击之怕打不倒，杀之怕刺不中。"

　　晏婴说："这三人只有勇敢，并无谋略。"

　　一天，鲁昭公到齐国访问。齐景公设宴招待，酒至半酣，侍者捧出鲜桃。鲜桃在齐国非常稀罕，宴席上只有五枚。一枚给鲁昭公，一枚给齐景公，一枚给晏婴。齐景公让晏婴将剩下的两枚鲜桃分给出席酒宴的三位勇士。

　　晏婴望着三位勇士说："你们当中谁的功劳最大，谁就应当吃一枚鲜桃。"

　　公孙接说："我应当吃一枚，主公打猎时，我杀死

merits," Yan Ying said, gazing at the three brave men. "Please tell me who deserves it."

"I deserve it," said Gongsun Jie. "I saved the duke's life when he was attacked by a boar during hunting."

Yan Ying promptly awarded him a peach along with a glass of wine.

Gu Yezi rose to his feet. "I am also entitled to one. Once I escorted the duke crossing a river. Suddenly a giant turtle sprang from under the water. Our boat was almost capsized. I jumped into the water, fought the animal and killed it. I nearly got drowned saving the duke's life."

Yan Ying awarded him a peach and a glass of wine.

Now the last one of the three warriors, Tian Kaijiang, stood up. "I saved the duke's life twice with my sword when he was attacked by the enemy in battle. Do you remember?"

"Yes, I do," said Yan Ying. "Your merits certainly top theirs, but you spoke too late. I can only offer you some wine now. But you'll be awarded a peach next year."

Tian Kaijiang was angry. "Killing a boar or a turtle is fine. But I fought the enemy to save the duke. Now I can't even have a peach, I'll be a laughing stock."

He drew out his sword and killed himself.

Gu Yezi was stunned. "I'm not as good as Tian Kaijiang. Now he is dead because I took the peach that really belongs to him. I hate myself. I would be a coward not to die."

Thus saying, he fell on his own sword.

Gongsun Jie looked on in consternation. "The three of us are always together. Now two are dead, what face have I got to live on?"

So he, too, cut his own throat.

COMMENT: A man of more muscle than brains invariably loses out to a man of more brains than muscle.

了一头野猪，救了主公一命。"

晏婴急忙进酒一杯，赐鲜桃一枚。

古冶之站了起来。"我也应当吃一枚。我曾护送主公过河。有一只大鼋从水中跃出，几乎把船打翻，我跳入水中，打死了大鼋。我冒着生命危险救了主公一命。"

晏婴忙进酒赐桃。

这时，田开疆站起来说："我曾两次手持兵器击退敌军，救了主公的命。你记得吗？"

晏婴说："我记得。将军的功劳最大，可惜你说得太迟了。我只能赏你一些酒，来年再给你鲜桃。"

田开疆大怒。"杀猪斩鼋不过是小事。我从敌军中把主公救出来，却吃不到一枚桃子，我会成为大家的笑柄。"

说完，他就拔剑自杀了。

古冶之惊呆了。"我的功劳不如田开疆。现在他死了，因为我吃了本来属于他的桃子。我恨自己，我没有脸活下去。"

说着，他也拔剑自杀了。

公孙接大惊失色。"我们三个人生死与共。现在，他们两人已经死了，我怎么有脸活下去呢？"

于是，他也刎颈自杀。

237

点评：头脑简单、四肢发达的人永远战胜不了头脑发达、四肢未必发达的人。

17

REVENGE IS SWEET

Sun Bin, a native of Qi, and Pang Juan, a native of Wei, were fellow students when they studied the art of war under Master of the Ghost Valley. Later Pang Juan became a successful general in Wei, but he knew his mastery of the art of war was not as good as Sun Bin's. If Sun Bin went to work for other countries he would pose a challenge to Wei. But if he came to Wei, he might threaten his own position as the king's right-hand man. Pang Juan turned the matter over in his mind and had an idea.

He invited Sun Bin to Wei and recommended him to the king. The king appointed him a senior advisor. Sun Bin was very grateful and took Pang Juan to be a trusty friend.

"How is your family in Qi?" Pang Juan asked him one day. "Why not bring them over?"

Sun Bin sighed. "My parents died when I was a child. I was brought up by my uncle. I have two cousins. But I've lost contact with them."

Half a year later, a man speaking with Qi accent came to see Sun Bin, bringing a letter from his cousins, in which they told him that his uncle had died and urged him to go back to Qi. The death of his uncle saddened Sun Bin, but given his position in the Wei court, he could not very well leave. So he wrote his cousin a letter and asked the visitor to carry it home. Unbeknownst to him, the letter was intercepted and handed to

17

孙膑复仇

孙膑是齐国人，庞涓是魏国人。两个人一块儿跟从鬼谷子学习兵法。后来庞涓做了魏国的大将。他知道孙膑的学问和本领都比自己强。如果孙膑给别的国家办事，就不好对付了。可是如果孙膑到魏国来，庞涓又怕自己的地位受到威胁。

庞涓左思右想，有了一个主意。他写了一封信给孙膑，请他到魏国来，并向魏王推荐了他。魏王任命孙膑为客卿。孙膑打心眼里感激庞涓，觉得他真够朋友。

有一天，庞涓问他："你家里人在齐国好吗？你怎么不把他们接来啊？"

孙膑叹了口气说："我父母早故了，从小由叔父养大。我有两个叔伯兄弟，可是不知道上哪里去了。"

过了半年光景，有个齐国口音的人来见孙膑，带了一封他叔伯哥哥的信，告诉他叔父已经死了，叫他快点回去。叔父的死使孙膑很悲伤。但是他在魏国做客卿，不便离开，就写了一封回信托来人带回去。没想到这封信被魏国人截获，交给了魏王。

魏王对庞涓说："孙膑想家，怎么办呢？"

the king.

"Sun Bin misses his home," the king said. "What shall we do?"

"He is a native of Qi," said Pang Juan. "It's only natural he wants to go back. But if he goes back and works in the Qi army, he can do us harm. Let me talk to him and ask him to stay."

Pang Juan asked Sun Bin about his visitor. "Why not ask the king for a leave of absence for a couple of months?" he suggested.

"I wanted to, but wouldn't I take too much liberty to ask the king for a home leave?"

"Not at all," Pang Juan assured him.

Shortly after he sent in his request, however, Sun Bin was arrested because the king suspected him of disloyalty. Pang Juan promised to intercede with the king, but when he came back from the court, he looked dejected. He told Sun Bin that the king wanted to put him to death. It was only after his mediation that the king agreed not to kill Sun Bin, but insisted on a severe punishment.

240

Madman

Sun Bin's face was tattooed and his knee-caps cut off. He was forbidden to leave Wei. The corporal punishment left him crippled. Pang Juan put him up in his own house and assigned an old servant to attend him.

Sun Bin was a descendant of Sun Tzu who wrote the famous book *The Art of War*. Pang Juan was eager to read the book. When he asked Sun Bin about it, Sun Bin said he had

庞涓说："父母之邦，谁能忘怀？不过，要是他回到齐国，当了齐国的将军，对我们就不利了。还是让我去劝劝他，请他留在这里吧。"

庞涓问了孙膑齐国访客的事，他说："你怎么不向大王请一两个月假呢？"

"我不是没有想过。可是我觉得向大王请假，太冒昧了。"

"你怕什么呢？"庞涓安慰他说。

孙膑就上了一个奏章，请假回齐国。魏王起了疑心，因而下令逮捕了他。庞涓答应向魏王求情。可是他从朝廷回来后，垂头丧气地告诉孙膑，魏王原来要定他死罪，只是因为庞涓求情，才保全了性命。可是孙膑必须受刑罚。

241

疯　　子

孙膑的脸上被刺了字，膝盖骨被剁掉，而且被禁止离开魏国。上刑后，孙膑变成了瘸子。庞涓让他住在自己家里，派了一个老仆人伺候他。

孙膑是《孙子兵法》的作者孙子的后代。庞涓急于想读《孙子兵法》。他问起时，孙膑说他早就把《孙子兵法》背得滚瓜烂熟，满口答应为庞涓默写这本兵书。庞涓听了很高兴。

learned the book by heart and would be happy to write it down for him. Pang Juan was very pleased.

Sun Bin's writing progressed slowly since he could not sit properly due to his injury. When Pang Juan heard he only wrote a few lines a day, he was upset.

"If he drags on like this, when will he finish the book?"

Sun Bin's servant learned from an aide of Pang Juan that Sun Bin was allowed to live only because Pang Juan wanted his book. As soon as he finished, he would be put to death.

The servant took pity on Sun Bin and told him the truth. It was like a bombshell. Sun Bin was so shocked he nearly fainted. When he came to, he threw all he had written into the fire. He felt he had awakened from a nightmare.

242

The next time Pang Juan came to see him, Sun Bin did not recognize him. He laughed and cried, and cried and laughed, and kept shouting at Pang Juan, "Help! Help!"

He has gone mad, Pang Juan thought. But he suspected Sun Bin of feigning insanity. So he had him dragged into a pig sty. Sun Bin fell onto a pile of pig dung, tossed about in the filth, and then fell into a stupor.

Pang Juan secretly sent a man to visit Sun Bin with some wine and food. Sun Bin threw away all the food and put some pig feces into his own mouth instead, claiming, "It's delicious!"

After that Pang Juan slackened surveillance on him. The pig sty became Sun Bin's home. In the day time, he would wander in the street. In the evening, he would come back to sleep. Sometimes he would sleep in the street. Everybody knew he was a sick man, but Pang Juan continued to spy on him.

One night as he was sleeping in the street, Sun Bin was wakened by a man. He recognized the man to be an old friend

孙膑因为身上的伤，无法坐直了写字，所以写的进度很慢，一天只能写三五行字。庞涓一听，冒了火。

"这么慢条斯理的，他要写到什么时候去？"

孙膑的仆人从庞涓跟前的人那里打听到，庞涓留着他的命，只是为了要他那部书。等到书写完了，他的命也就完了。

仆人同情孙膑，就把真相告诉了他。孙膑肝胆俱裂，几乎闭过气去。等到缓过气后，他把写好的兵书统统扔到火里烧了。他觉得自己仿佛从一场噩梦中醒来。

庞涓来见孙膑时，孙膑一会儿哭，一会儿笑，一个劲地冲着他喊："救命啊！救命啊！"

庞涓心想，孙膑疯了，又怕他装疯，就叫人把他揪到猪圈里。孙膑倒在粪堆上，打了几个滚，就睡着了。

庞涓暗地里派人给他送酒饭。孙膑把送来的酒饭都倒在地下，抓了一把猪粪往嘴里塞，还连说好吃。

打这时起，庞涓就放松了对他的监视。孙膑住在猪圈里。白天，他爬到外面去；晚上，又爬回来睡觉。有时候，他就躺在街上过夜。人人都知道孙膑是个疯子。庞涓仍旧派人监视着他。

一天夜里，孙膑躺在街上，有人叫醒了他。孙膑认出来人是齐国的一位老友。这人告诉孙膑，齐国的使臣来魏国访问，有意偷偷将他带回齐国。孙膑说，庞涓天天派人看着他。老友叫一个手下人换上孙膑的衣服，假

from Qi. The man told him that an envoy from Qi was visiting Wei and wanted to smuggle him out of the country.

Sun Bin said he was being watched by Pang Juan's men. Thereupon his friend had one of his subordinates change into Sun Bin's clothes to take his place in the street. The next day Sun Bin, hidden in the carriage of Qi's envoy, escaped from Wei. Two days later, Sun Bin's impersonator disappeared. Pang Juan ordered an immediate search, but to no avail.

Horse Race

When Sun Bin arrived in Qi, General Tian Ji invited him to stay in his house. Knowing Sun Bin was well-versed in the art of war, the general held him in great respect.

Tian Ji liked gambling on horse races with the king and other noblemen. But he was often a loser. Sun Bin noticed that the racehorses were divided into three classes and their quality did not differ much within the same class.

He asked General Tian to bet heavily on the next race. "I guarantee you will win."

Tian Ji put down a thousand ounces of gold betting against the king. In the first round of the race, Sun Bin told him to use his third class horse to compete with the king's first class horse. In the second round, Sun Bin told him to use his first class against the king's second class. Then in the final round, his second class was made to run against the king's third class. Tian Ji lost the first round but won the next two. The king lost a thousand ounces of gold.

Tian Ji introduced Sun Bin to the king after the race. Sun

装孙膑躺在街上。第二天，孙膑藏在齐国使臣的车子里，逃离了魏国。过了两天，那个假扮孙膑的人不见了。庞涓立即下令搜寻，却不见孙膑的踪影。

赛　马

孙膑到了齐国，大将田忌请他住在家里。田忌知道孙膑熟谙兵法，视他为上宾。

田忌喜欢赛马，常和齐王跟王室贵族比赛。可是他常常输。孙膑观察了几次，发现出场的马分为上中下三个等级。同一等级的马相差无几。

他告诉田忌："下一次赛马多下点赌注，我保证你获胜。"

田忌和齐王又赛马时，下注一千两金子。头一场比赛，孙膑叫田忌把三等马跟齐王的头等马比。第二场比赛，孙膑让田忌用头等马跟齐王的二等马比。第三场，用二等马跟齐王的三等马比。田忌输了第一场，却连赢第二、第三场。齐王输掉了一千两金子。

比赛结束后，田忌将孙膑介绍给齐王。孙膑向齐王解释了他制胜的计策。齐王非常佩服，就拜他为军师。

孙膑打发人去打听叔伯哥哥的消息。哪里找得到这两个人呢？他这才明白，那个带齐国口音的送信人，原

Bin explained how he had helped the general to win. The king was much impressed and appointed him to be his senior military advisor.

Sun Bin made an inquiry about his uncle and cousins. They were nowhere to be found. He realized that the man with Qi accent was a phony. The letter and the news of his uncle's death were all part of Pang Juan's trick.

Besieging the Besieger

In 354 B.C. Pang Juan led an army of 80,000 and besieged Handan, the capital of Zhao. The ruler of Zhao asked for help from Qi. The king of Qi intended to appoint Sun Bin as commander to lead an army to Zhao's rescue. Sun Bin declined because he felt as a convict in Wei, it would not be appropriate for him to assume that position. So he became General Tian Ji's top advisor for the mission.

He dissuaded Tian Ji from going to Zhao. "Right now the best troops of Wei are in Zhao. Only the weak ones are left to defend their homeland. If we invade Wei, cut the supply lines of its army, and overrun its military positions where defense is weak, Pang Juan will be forced to pull back his army. Then the siege of Handan will be lifted."

Pang Juan's troops were about to overrun Zhao's capital when news came that Wei's stronghold Xiangling was besieged by Qi. Pang Juan had to stop his attack and bring his troops home. But those besieging Xiangling were only part of the Qi army. Another force of Qi was waiting for the Wei army on its way home. The ambush was a great success. Wei lost more than 20,000 men and was forced to make peace with Zhao.

来是冒充的。家信和叔父的死全是庞涓使的鬼主意。

围魏救赵

　　公元前 354 年，庞涓率八万大军进攻赵国，围困了国都邯郸。赵国的国君向齐王求救。齐王要拜孙膑为大将去救赵国。孙膑推辞说自己是魏国的罪人，当大将不合适。于是，齐王拜田忌为大将，拜孙膑为军师，发兵去救赵国。

　　孙膑建议田忌不去赵国。他说："目前魏国的精兵都在赵国。只有老兵弱将留在国内。如果我们攻打魏国，切断魏军的补给线，打下几个防卫薄弱的城镇，庞涓听到，一定往回跑，这样，就可以解赵都之围。"

　　庞涓的军队正要攻进邯郸，突然听说齐国的军队包围了重镇襄陵。他立刻停止进攻，退兵回国救援。但是，包围襄陵的只是一部分齐军。另一支齐军在半路等待魏军。齐军伏击获胜，魏军损失了两万多士兵，不得不跟赵国讲和。

247

Camp-fire

A few years later, Wei's army invaded Han. Han was a small kingdom. Too weak to defend itself, Han appealed to Qi for help. Sun Bin was in favor of rendering Han assistance, but suggested that Qi's army not go into battle prematurely.

"Qi's army should fight for Qi's interest. If we go there too early, we would be doing the fighting for Han. The best is let Han fight Wei first. After both sides are exhausted, then we can commit our forces to the battle."

As Sun Bin had predicted, the morale of Han's troops was boosted when they learned that Qi would come to their rescue. But they were no match for Wei's offensive and the situation became desperate. Pang Juan was on the point of routing Han's force when he learned the army of Qi had invaded Wei. He was forced to pull back his troops. His bitter experience in Zhao gnawing at his heart, he was determined to fight it out with Sun Bin.

Sun Bin ordered his army to retreat and Pang Juan pursued. On the way, Sun Bin had camp-fires for 100,000 men built on the first day, camp-fires for 50,000 men built on the second day and on the third day camp-fires for 30,000 men were built.

Pang Juan always regarded the army of Wei as the best in the world and looked down upon others. He was delighted to find that the number of camp-fires of the Qi army was declining by each passing day.

"I know Qi's troops are no good," he said. "That's why more than half of their soldiers deserted the army in three days."

To speed up, he formed a crack force of lightly armed men to run after his opponent.

减 灶 法

几年后，魏军进攻韩国。韩国是一个小国，没有力量保卫自己，就向齐国求救。孙膑虽然赞成搭救韩国，但主张齐军不必立即参战。

"齐军是为齐国的利益出战的。如果我们去早了，我们等于为韩国作战。最好是让韩军抵抗魏军，等到双方厮杀，实力消耗后，再出兵不迟。"

果然不出孙膑所料，韩军知道有齐军相救，士气大振。但是，毕竟弱不胜强，军情危急。庞涓就要击溃韩军的时候，得到齐国攻打魏国的告急信，只好撤兵回国。庞涓对上次在赵国的惨败记忆犹新。这次，他下决心与孙膑决一雌雄。

孙膑下令齐军后撤。庞涓紧追不舍。在退兵途中，第一天，孙膑下令在营地造供十万人吃饭用的炉灶。第二天，他下令造供五万人吃的炉灶。第三天，他下令造仅供三万人吃的炉灶。

庞涓向来认为魏军是天下最悍勇的军队，而看不起别国的军队。当他发现齐军的营地炉灶每天减少，就得意地说："我知道齐军不行，才二天工夫，就逃了一大半。"

为了追上齐军，他亲自率领一支精兵，轻装前进。

Maling

Sun Bin reckoned that Pang Juan's army would arrive at a place called Maling on the evening of the fourth day. The road to Maling was narrow and there were mountains on both sides. Sun Bin had five hundred picked archers hidden by the road. They were to shoot the instant they saw a flame. He had all the trees felled down to block the passage except for a tall one which was stripped of its bark to bear the words written in black ink.

"Pang Juan shall die under this tree."

Pang Juan arrived at Maling on time as Sun Bin had expected. But fallen trees blocked the way and his men had to remove them. No doubt Sun Bin was trying to slow him down. Then he noticed a tall tree standing alone and something was written on its exposed trunk, but it was too dark to see. Pang Juan lit a torch. As soon as he saw what was written on it, he realized he had walked into a trap. But it was too late. Barely had he issued an order to retreat when arrows came down like rain.

"The bastard—I should have killed him," he growled before he breathed his last. "Now he's going to make a name at my expense."

The army of Qi won a decisive victory.

COMMENT: If Sun Bin had only endurance but not iron will, he would not have survived. If he had only will power but not the knowledge of the art of war, he could not have wrought his revenge. The combination of these qualities made Sun Bin one of the most intriguing figures in Chinese history. Like his ancestor Sun Tzu, Sun Bin also wrote a book on the art of war which was discovered in 1972. It was another classic on the subject.

马陵道上

孙膑预计庞涓的军队在第四天日暮必抵达马陵。马陵道是一条狭窄的道路，夹在两座山的中间。孙膑挑选了五百名弓弩手，埋伏在山路两旁。吩咐他们当夜一发现火光，就一齐放箭。他命令将士们把路旁的树全部砍掉，堵住道路，只留一棵最大的没有砍，刮去一段树皮，写了几个大字：庞涓死于此树下。

果然不出孙膑所料，庞涓按时到达马陵。但是，山道给断树堵住，难以前行。士兵不得不搬木开路。显然，孙膑是怕魏军追上。

庞涓发现山下剩下一棵孤零零的树，树身上隐隐有字迹，但昏暗难辨。他点起火来，看个分明，才知道自己中了计，就立即下令退兵，但已经来不及了。无数支箭像雨点一般冲他射来。

庞涓临死前恨恨地说："我后悔没有杀了这畜牲！现在他要成名了。"

这一仗，齐军取得了决定性胜利。

251

点评：如果孙膑只有忍耐力，而没有铁一般的意志，他就不可能活下来。如果他只有意志力，而不懂得兵法，他也不可能为自己复仇。孙膑所具备的这些特点使他成为中国历史上最富有传奇色彩的人物之一。继他的先辈孙子之后，孙膑也写了一部兵法。这部兵法于1972年被发现，成为中国兵书中又一本经典著作。

PART VI

WISDOM OF *THE BOOK OF CHANGES*

《易经》的管理智慧

The Book of Changes has been consulted by millions for thousands of years as a manual of divination. Its authorship is attributed to Fu Xi, the sage ruler of China nearly five thousand years ago, with King Wen, founder of the Zhou dynasty, Duke of Zhou, his son, and Confucius providing subsequent expansion and interpretation.

But *The Book of Changes* is more than a prognostication tool. Confucius said: "Sage kings of antiquity sought guidance from *The Book of Changes* in carrying out the will of the people, in laying the foundation of their great enterprises, and in forming judgment in times of difficulty and uncertainty."

Embedded its mysterious oracle is a philosophy that has become part and parcel of Chinese wisdom. In the following, we shall explore the underlying messages of its sixty-four hexagrams to see what the book has to say about the qualities a man should cultivate and the actions he should take during the different phases of his career.

人们用《易经》占卜吉凶已有几千年了。《易经》相传是中国五千年前的圣人伏羲所作。后经周朝的创始者周文王、文王的儿子周公和孔子加以扩充和解释。

但是《易经》的功用远不止占卜。孔子说，圣人用《易经》"以通天下之志，以定天下之业，以断天下之疑"。

《易经》蕴含的哲理是中国智慧的一个组成部分。以下我们将探讨《易经》的六十四个卦，看看一个成功者应当具备什么素质，以及一个人在生涯的不同阶段应当如何自处。

小
xiǎo
small

此字在表示"分开"的意思的"八"字当中加一条直线，表示将一样东西分成两半，它就变小了。

"八" means to divide. Adding a vertical line in the middle conveys the sense that if something is divided into two halves, it is bound to become smaller.

1

THE SUCCESS QUALITIES

(1) A good leader inspires his followers with noble character and exemplary conduct. He is tolerant and magnanimous. He selects worthy men to work for him and never stoops to trickery.

(2) Be sincere, and you will find an echo in people's heart. Be sincere, and you will win their trust. Be sincere, and success will come your way, for this is the Way of Heaven.

(3) Good relationship cannot be forced. If you are sincere and your motives worthy, virtuous men will rally around you.

(4) Good relationship evolves naturally. It is like the interaction between a man and a woman. It is easy for the relationship to blossom if you are honest, gentle, responsive and open-minded.

(5) Be humble. A humble leader wins the support of the people. But humbleness must be backed by substance. Humbleness does not mean holding yourself back when firm action is called for.

(6) Humbleness does not mean self-abasement or indecisiveness. Humbleness means prudence. Be prudent before the event and prudent after the event.

(7) Be cheerful, and you will make others cheerful too. Cheerfulness is conducive to harmony. Be genuinely pleasing but be not obsequious. And be wary of those who fawn on you.

(8) Good etiquette cultivates good behavior. No

1

成功的素质

（临）优秀的领导以身作则，以高尚的人格感召下属。他待人宽容，敦厚而不苛刻。他选拔贤能，而从不以诱骗为手段。

（中孚）有诚信就能引起人们的共鸣；有诚信就能得到人们的信任；有诚信就能取得成功，因为诚信符合天道。

（比）人际关系不可强求。如果你心中诚信，动机纯正，贤明高尚的人就会团结在你周围。

（咸）人际关系是自然发展的，就像男女之间的关系一样。如果你以诚相待、和风细雨、心胸宽大、善于沟通、敏于感应，就容易建立良好的人际关系。

（谦）要谦虚。一个谦虚的领导将赢得人们的支持。但谦虚必须有实质。谦虚绝不意味在需要果断行动的时候退让不前。

（巽）谦虚并非自我贬低或优柔寡断。谦虚意味着慎重，意味着事前周详考虑和事后检讨得失的慎重态度。

（兑）你自己喜悦也会使别人喜悦。喜悦能使人际关系和谐。但取悦于人不等于阿谀奉承。应当警惕那些

organization can run smoothly without good manners. But do not let good manners become mere formalities. Real good manners spring from good morals.

(9) If you want an inexhaustible supply of water, dig your well in a good site and maintain it properly. If you want talented men to keep coming to you, seek them assiduously and make the best use of them.

(10) If you have integrity, you will have loyal followers. If you are committed, you will have committed followers. Bring together like minds to work with you for a common objective, and you will succeed.

(11) Give good training to those work for you. Teach them. Enlighten them. Remember teaching benefits the teacher, too.

(12) Managing an enterprise is like managing a household. The head of the household should perform his duty and set a good example to others. He should be kind and caring but also strict, and he should never be indulgent.

(13) Your outward conduct reflects your inner world. Take time to examine yourself. Watch how others react to what you say and what you do. If you understand how you are being perceived, you'll know how to conduct yourself.

拍马逢迎的小人。

（贲） 文明的礼仪能培养文明的行为，一个不讲礼貌的组织是无法顺利运转的。但不要将礼貌流于外表的形式。只有重品德、重内涵的礼貌才是好礼貌。

（井） 如果你希望获得源源不断的供水，就要择地掘井，细加维护。如果你希望得到源源不断的人才，就要发掘人才，并充分发挥他们的才能。

（萃） 你品德高尚，下面的人就对你忠诚。你意志坚定，下面的人就有决心。如果你能够团结志同道合之士，为共同的目标而奋斗，你就一定会成功。

（蒙） 要好好地培训下属，好好地教育他们、启发他们。须知：教学相长。

259

（家人） 治理企业如同治家。做家长的应该以身作则，做好本分工作。既要慈爱关怀，又要严格要求。千万不能纵容溺爱。

（观） 你的一举一动反映了你的内心世界。你要经常自我反省。留意别人对你的言行如何反应。如果你了解别人如何看待你，你就知道应该如何表现自己。

2

THE BEGINNING PHASE

(14) The beginning phase is full of perils as well as potentials. You must be resolute, fear no hardships, press ahead and persevere. But do not act blindly.

(15) You are not equal to your task yet. Store up your energy and resources. Joining forces with like minds. Make preparations for success.

(16) Build up your enterprise gradually. Make steady but sure progress according to your capability. Don't make premature moves. A tall tree has deep roots; it grows slowly.

(17) If you have to accept a subordinate position, make a virtue of necessity. Make the best of it. Keep up your spirit.

(18) Be a good subordinate. Be obedient but keep your integrity intact. Be as generous and broad-minded as the earth is.

(19) Sometimes you should set aside your own interest to follow others for the sake of unity and harmony. Don't be short-sighted, for harmony bears fruits.

(20) Put the interests of the group above the individual. Seek consensus on big issues and don't fuss about minor differences. Unity is strength and harmony is bliss.

(21) Don't shun those who differ from you or even oppose you. It is in your interest to communicate with them and seek common ground.

2

开始阶段

（屯）开始阶段既充满生机，也充满危机。你必须意志坚定，不畏艰险，锲而不舍，积极进取，但不要盲目行动。

（小畜）此时你心有余而力不足，需要积蓄力量，联合志同道合之士携手并进，为成功做准备。

（渐）要循序渐进，量力而行，稳中求胜，不要急于求成。树高根必深。一棵大树是渐渐长成的，绝非一朝一夕之功。

（归妹）如果你是别人的下属，就要随遇而安，把工作做好。要乐观向上，好好利用这一机会。

（坤）作为下属要服从上级，也要德行方正。要效法大地，以宽厚的德行容纳他人。

（随）有时候应放弃一己之私利，跟随他人，以维护团结和谐。须知：和气生财。切勿贪图近利。

（同人）群体的利益高于个人的利益。与人合作，应求大同存小异。团结是力量；和气是吉祥。

（睽）不要回避那些有不同意见甚至反对你的人。要主动地跟他们沟通，异中求同。这样做，对你只有好处，

(22) Promote those who are honest and capable; remove those who are mean and unfit. A wise leader and worthy followers bring out the best from each other.

(23) Be patient and have faith. Keep away from dangers. Go with the flow of the tide. Take the tide at the flood to carry out your plan.

(24) Act cautiously as though you were walking behind a tiger. Be aware of risks and don't be foolhardy. Be aware of your limitations and don't overreach yourself.

没有坏处。

（鼎）重用贤能。摒弃小人和不称职者。做领导的，知人善用，才能上下同心，相得益彰。

（需）要有耐心、有信心。要远离危险，以免遭祸。要顺潮而动，等待时机，实现你的计划。

（履）行动时要小心谨慎，就像跟在老虎后面那样，要有戒惧心。应该有风险意识，不可刚愎自用。应该量力而行，不可逞强冒进。

少
shǎo
few; less

"小"字加上一撇，表示数量少。
Adding a stroke to "小" conveys the sense of cutting something smaller and making it less.

3

THE DIFFICULT PHASE

(25) You are bound to encounter obstacles, but you must hold the course. Seek support from like minds. Seek help from distinguished men.

(26) Those who are in positions of power can help you. But be careful whom you turn to. Attach yourself to the worthy. Be open and above-board. Don't be opportunistic.

(27) Tackle a difficult problem early on. Don't let it impede your progress. Be thorough in weeding out bad elements. Take drastic measures if necessary.

(28) No gains without pains. No difficulty can be solved without paying a price. Make sure people understand why they have to make sacrifices.

(29) Do not use improper means to solve your problem, or you will get yourself into deeper trouble. Hold fast to your principles, and you will have no regret. Stick to the right path in adversity, and fortune will smile upon you.

(30) An extraordinary situation calls for extraordinary action. A crisis requires crisis management. Be cautious, but don't be afraid if you have to act alone. Do not let the criticism of others affect you.

(31) Be firm and fearless in the face of dangers and difficulties, but be not reckless. Be sure to preserve yourself. And then explore ways and means of surmounting difficulties.

3

困难阶段

（蹇）你一定会遇到困难，但决不可退缩。要寻求志同道合之士的支持；寻求贵人相助。

（离）有权势的人能在困难的时候帮助你。但是，你必须谨慎选择求助的对象。只能依附于贤者。要光明磊落，不可投机取巧。

（解）在困难开始的时候，就要迅速解决，不要让它妨碍你。除恶务尽。对小人在必要的时候应采取断然手段予以打击。

（损）解决困难，必然要付出代价。有得必有损。应当让大家理解为什么要做出牺牲。

（困）解决困难的手段必须正当，否则你会陷入更深的困境。只有坚持原则，你将来才不会后悔。只要在逆境中恪守正道，你就一定会得到幸运之神的眷顾。

（大过）对付非常情况，要使用非常手段；对付危机，要采取危机管理。应当极其慎重，但不必害怕独自行动，不必顾忌他人的批评。

（坎）在险难的环境中，要坚定刚强，不要轻举妄动。应先求自保，然后寻求突破险境的途径。

(32) If you inherit a situation that has fallen into decay, focus on the future. Don't dwell on the past but examine the causes of decay. Initiate reform and persevere. You can turn it around.

(33) Be on guard against mean men. They must be contained, or they will influence other people. Don't associate yourself with mean men even if you are isolated and cut off from help.

(34) When mean men are in the ascendant, it is a time for non-action. Never associate with them. Let things take their own course. Let things right themselves.

(35) When mean men hold sway, keep yourself out of harm's way. Don't despair. Nothing lasts forever.

(36) The darkest hours may be the best time to prepare for success. The safest place may be near the source of danger. Lie low and bide your time.

(37) Retreat when the forces of darkness are overwhelming. Or you may cause harm to yourself. Retreat to preserve your strength. Retreat in order to advance.

(38) Bad things can happen to good people. Even if you have done nothing wrong, you may still have bad luck. Concentrate on sowing and plowing rather than worrying about the harvest.

（蛊）挽救败局，应着眼于将来。谴责过去无益，但必须找出造成败局的原因。彻底革新，坚持下去，才能挽狂澜于既倒，重振旗鼓。

（姤）对小人要戒备，要遏制，否则他们会影响其他人。即使你孤立无援，也不可与小人结伴。

（剥）小人得势之际，君子不宜行动。不可与小人同流合污。不妨让事物自我发展，自我纠正。

（否）小人势长时，君子应避免遭受伤害，不作无谓的牺牲。不要绝望，因为黑暗不可能长久。

（明夷）最黑暗的时候往往是为成功打基础的最佳时候。最危险的场所往往是最安全的地方。应韬光养晦，等待时机。

267

（遁）黑暗势力猖獗的时候，君子应当退隐，否则会徒然受到伤害。要以退为进，保存好自己，以便日后再起。

（无妄）好人也有无妄之灾。没做错事也会碰到坏运气。应当只问耕耘，不问收获。当为则为，尽其在我。

4

THE GROWTH PHASE

(39) The tree has taken deep roots and broken up the soil. It is the season of growth. Now you have done all the groundwork, go forward confidently. Do not hesitate. Do not waver or worry.

(40) Now you are strong enough to clear away all obstacles in your way. Exercise your power with caution, or you will be overbearing. Temper your strength with restraint, or you will cause resentment.

(41) Crime must be rooted out. Bad behavior must be punished. If a small evil is not eradicated, it can turn into a disaster. But be fair in meting out punishment.

(42) Devise a surefire action plan and wait for the appropriate moment to eliminate evildoers. Smash them at one blow. Don't give them time to react.

(43) If you underestimate your capability, you may not fully realize your potential. But if you overestimate your capability, you may bring disaster upon yourself.

(44) Do not panic when an emergency arises or you'll make things worse. Stay calm and collected. Do your best to minimize the damage. Draw a lesson from the disaster.

(45) If you make a mistake, correct it quickly. If you deviate from the right path, come back right away. Don't make the same mistake twice.

4

成长阶段

（升）树木已经生根破土。成长的季节已经来临。你已经打下了基础。现在可以充满信心地前进。不必疑虑，不必彷徨。

（大壮）现在你有力量扫除前进道路上的一切障碍。但用力必须得当，不要盛气凌人。必须自我克制，免得遭人忌恨。

（噬嗑）犯罪必须根除；恶劣的行为必须受到惩罚。小恶如不杜绝，就会酿成灾祸。但惩罚要公正。

（夬）消除邪恶分子，应有万全的策划和准备，不可妄动。要把握时机，一举歼灭，不给他们以反击的机会。

（小过）过低估计自己的能力，可能使你没有充分发挥潜质。但过高估计自己的能力，可能给你带来灾难。

（震）遭遇突发事件时，不要惊慌失措，否则会更加糟糕。要镇定从容，临危不惧，最大限度地减少损失。并从中吸取教训。

（复）犯了错误，就要及时改正。误入歧途，就要迅速回到正道上来。不要重蹈覆辙，一错再错。

（讼）争论的目的是得出正确的结论，而不是为了

(46) The purpose of argument is to get the truth, not for the sake of winning the argument. The purpose of negotiation is to get the cooperation of the other party. Make concessions when necessary.

(47) If war cannot be avoided, make sure you have the support of the people. Appoint experienced men as commanders. Never place mean men in positions of importance.

(48) Perseverance is essential to achieving your goal. Constancy of purpose enables you to endure hardships. Stand firm but avoid extremes in your action. The golden mean is the right path and the right path leads you to success.

(49) The sun is shining on your horizon. March forward with all your strength. Bring out all that is best in you and let people follow you.

争赢。谈判的目的是得到对方的合作，必要时应作出让步。

（师）如果非打仗不可，就必须得到民众的支持。要派有经验的人指挥作战，绝不可重用小人。

（恒）有恒方能有成。目标坚定，你就不畏艰险。你要坚持立场，但做起事来，应把握中庸的原则，不要走极端。中庸之道将指引你走向成功。

（晋）阳光照亮了大地。你要全力以赴，勇往直前，以身作则，让民众跟随你。

271

劣
liè
bad; inferior

此字将"少"和"力"放在一起，意思是如果在工作中出力少，结果自然不会好。
The character combines "less" ("少") with "strength" ("力") conveys the sense that if you do not work hard, you will get inferior result.

5

THE SUCCESS PHASE

(50) The closer you get to success, the riskier things can be. One step short of success still means failure. Be extremely careful. Sustain your effort until you have attained your goal.

(51) As you reap the harvest of your success, don't let it turn your head. Remain humble and tolerant. Be sincere and make as many friends as you can.

(52) Be sure to share the joy of success with others. Let your enthusiasm draw others to you. But don't get carried away.

(53) The accumulation of wealth should be matched by the accumulation of virtue and wisdom. Don't be greedy. Too much wealth can be negative.

(54) There is a time to advance and a time to stop. Stop before going too far, and you will have no regret.

(55) Wealth gives you resources to support others as well as yourself. Give back to society what you have received from it. Good intention and good deeds bring you good luck.

(56) The more you give, the more you will receive. The goodwill you generate will boost your cause. The support you get will push you to greater success.

(57) Now you have attained your goal, don't be complacent. You must continue to work hard to keep your success.

5

成功阶段

（未济）越是接近成功，就越有危险。走错一步路，就会功亏一篑。在关键时刻，千万不可掉以轻心。要坚持到底，直到完成目标。

（大有）享受胜利果实的时候，不要让成功冲昏头脑。要礼贤下士，以诚信结交天下。

（豫）要跟他人分享胜利的喜悦，让你的热情感染他人，但不可沉溺于喜乐之中。

（大畜）积财的同时，也要积德和积累智慧。不要贪财，财富过多并非好事。

（艮）当进则进，当停则停。不知适可而止的人，日后必定后悔。

（颐）财富给予你既能供养自己又能帮助他人的资源。应当取之于民，用之于民。积德积善者，大吉大利。

（益）施得越多，得到的也越多。你帮助别人，就会得到别人的支持，就会拥有更多的力量，获得更大的成就。

（既济）创业已告成功，但不可骄傲自满。为了保持成功，你要继续奋发努力。

6

THE RENEWAL PHASE

(58) Achieving success is not easy; keeping it is even harder. Keep up the momentum in times of peace and prosperity. Do not rest on your laurels. The seeds of decline are planted in the peak of triumph.

(59) Prosperity tends to corrupt people's morals, sap their morale, and divide them. A wise leader takes prompt action to stop the tendency.

(60) Going too far is as bad as not going far enough. Misfortune awaits those who commit excesses. Exercise restraint in what you say and what you do.

(61) Danger happens when you think you are safe. Decline begins when you think your prosperity will last long. Disorder sets in when you believe you live in peace.

(62) Change is the law of the universe. Things tend to move in cycle and when they become extreme, they will move in the opposite direction, and then the cycle of events will start all over again. The gentleman conforms to the will of Heaven. Just as Heaven makes constant motion to renew itself, so the gentleman makes unceasing effort to improve himself.

(63) Prosperity is hard to sustain. Things can be unstable again. Don't lose sight of your goal. Be humble, seek help from others, and you will advance your cause to a new height.

(64) When corruption sets in, it is time to reform. If you

6

革新阶段

（泰）创业固然艰难，守成更加不易。在和平繁荣时期，也要力求继续发展，不能吃老本。须知：盛极必衰。

（涣）生活安逸的时候，道德容易下滑，斗志容易削弱，人心容易涣散。一个聪明的领导会采取行动，及时制止这种趋势。

（节）过犹不及。一个不知节制的人一定会遭遇不幸。要谨言慎行，才能持盈保泰。

（丰）危险往往发生在你以为是安全的时候。衰败往往起源于你以为是繁荣的时候。动乱往往出现在你以为是太平的时候。

（乾）变化是宇宙的法则。事物的发展，周而复始，循环不已，物极必反，盛极而衰。君子处事顺应天意。天行健，君子以自强不息。

（旅）步入盛况以后，又会陷入新的不安定状态。要牢记你的目标是什么。以谦虚的态度寻求他人的支持，就能将事业推向新的高度。

（革）腐败产生之际，就是实行改革之时。必须使人们相信改革的出路是光明的，才能得到他们的支持，才

convince the people that reform will lead to a bright future, they will support you and adapt themselves to the new life in the wake of the reform.

COMMENT: *The Book of Changes* deals with the changing phases of life. It tells us there is a time to create, a time to grow, and a time to enjoy the fruits of your labor. There is also a time to retreat, a time to lie low, and a time to guard against decline.

Knowing what phase you are in and acting accordingly will stand you in good stead. It will help you survive in bad time and lead you to success in good time. It will make you emotionally intelligent so that you won't be depressed when things seem to go against you, for you know it will pass in time. Nor will you get carried away on the pinnacle of triumph, for you know it won't last forever.

Some events you can influence; others are simply out of your control. No matter what phase you are in, *the Book of Changes* advises you to be humble, tolerant, keep integrity and stick to the golden mean.

能使他们适应改革成功后的新的生活。

点评：《易经》阐述的是人生不同阶段需要把握的要谛。我们做每件事都要当其时。要知道你什么时候是创造期，什么时候是成长期，什么时候应享受劳动的果实。也要知道什么时候应当以退为进，什么时候应当韬光养晦，什么时候需要防止盛极而衰。

如果你知道自己处于哪一个阶段，并且采取相应的行动，就能趋吉避凶，使你在不利的时候生存下来，在有利的时候走向成功；使你在逆境中不会灰心丧气，因为你知道逆境是暂时的；使你在成功时不会得意忘形，因为你知道成功也不是永久的。

人生有些事物你能够施加影响，有些事物你根本无法掌控。不管你的人生处于哪一个阶段，《易经》谆谆告诫你必须谦虚、宽容、正直、遵循中庸之道。

277

尖
jiān
pointed;
sharp

此字上部是小字，下部是大字，表示从大渐小。
The upper part of the ideograph means small and the lower part big.
It describes something tapering from big to small.

A NOTE ON PRONUNCIATION

The romanization of Chinese names presents some difficulty. This book adopts the pinyin system, the official phonetic alphabet in China, but some proper names such as Confucius, Lao Tzu, Sun Tzu and Yangtze are spelled in their traditional way according to the Wade-Giles system because Western readers are already familiar with them.

278 Most of the letters in the pinyin system are pronounced more or less as what the English reader would expect, but there are a few baffling exceptions: *c* sounds like *ts* as in *cuts*, *q* like *ch* as in *chin*, *x* like *sh* as in *she* and *zh* like *j* as in *Joe*.

图书在版编目(CIP)数据

中国智慧故事.1，管理智慧篇：汉英对照/唐庆华著.
上海：上海人民出版社，2008
ISBN 978－7－208－07831－4

Ⅰ.中... Ⅱ.唐... Ⅲ.①英语-汉语-对照读物②故事-
作品集-中国-当代 Ⅳ.H319.4：Ⅰ

中国版本图书馆 CIP 数据核字(2008)第 050489 号

责任编辑　张玲雅
封面装帧　袁银昌

中国智慧故事（一）：管理智慧篇
（英汉对照）
唐庆华 著
世 纪 出 版 集 团
上海人民出版社出版
(200001　上海福建中路 193 号　www.ewen.cc)
世纪出版集团发行中心发行
上海锦佳装璜印刷发展公司印刷
开本 890×1240　1/32　印张 9.25　插页 3　字数 157,000
2008 年 8 月第 1 版　2008 年 8 月第 1 次印刷
ISBN 978－7－208－07831－4/K・1440
定价 30.00 元

About The Book of Chinese Wisdom

Book I Art of Management

Book I gleans nearly seventy tales of the art of management. With China's long tradition of civil administration, management was a refined art in ancient China. Management, in essence, is about people. Despite advances in science and technology, human nature has hardly changed since ancient times. The wisdom embedded in these tales will strike the reader as both fresh and practical. Book I also explores the wisdom of *The Book of Changes* from a business perspective.

Book II Wit and Humor

Book II gleans about seventy tales of wit and humor. Through them the reader will find that wisdom manifests itself in many ways. It can mean the enlightenment of the mind, a sound philosophy of living, a stratagem, or the effective management of a difficult situation. This volume contains many fables whose moral has become an integral part of Chinese wisdom. A dozen well-known stories of Zen are also included.

Book III Virtues and Values

Confucianism is not only China's cultural heritage but a vital part of Chinese wisdom. In Book III we shall find out what kind of a man Confucius was like. We shall also learn the wisdom of Lao Tzu, an older contemporary of Confucius. A traditional Chinese family often had a set of precepts that served as rules of conduct for everybody to follow. They occupy a special place in Chinese culture. In Book III we shall present two well-known examples of familial precepts.

Book IV Power and Influence

The period between the fall of an old dynasty and the rise of a new one seems to be the best focal point to observe the folly and wisdom of man. The times gave birth to great men whose talent and wisdom were brought into full swing by fate. Book IV examines three most significant periods in Chinese history. The first is the rise of the Qin dynasty and its rapid collapse; the second is the rise of the Han dynasty; and the third is the downfall of the Ming dynasty and the rise of the Qing.

《中国智慧故事》 分册简介

第一册　管理智慧篇

第一册搜集了近七十个有关管理艺术的故事。中国悠久的文职传统使管理在古代就已经成为一门练达的艺术。管理艺术是与人打交道的艺术。今天，尽管科学技术取得了长足的进步，但是人的本性几乎没有变化。读者将发现本书故事里的智慧既新鲜又实用。本书还从管理角度探讨了《易经》的智慧。

第二册　机智幽默篇

第二册搜集了近七十个饱蘸机智和幽默的故事。读者将发现，智慧的表达方式多种多样。它可以指心灵的觉悟，可以指一种健全的人生哲学，也可以指一种智谋，或者一种应对棘手局面的方法。本书许多寓言的哲理是中国智慧的一个重要组成部分。本书还收了一些著名的禅宗的故事。

第三册　教育伦理篇

儒教不仅是中国的文化遗产，也是中国智慧的一个不可或缺的组成部分。第三册将介绍孔子的生平和为人，还将介绍孔子的同时代人——老子的智慧。传统的中国家庭往往有一部家训作为家族成员的行为准则。治家格言在中国文化中有特殊的位置。本书将介绍两部著名的古代治家格言。

第四册　权谋兵法篇

观察人的智慧和愚蠢的最佳时期似乎是当一个旧王朝为一个新王朝所取代的那段时期。伟人往往产生在这段时期里。命运让他们有机会尽其智慧，施展才华。本书考察了中国历史上三个最有意义的时期。第一个是秦朝的崛起和崩溃的过程；第二个是汉朝兴起的过程；第三个是明末清初的动荡年代。